THE BLOOD LETTER

HOW A YOUNG WOMAN SURVIVED FOUR SOVIET EAST GERMAN PRISONS

HELGA E. RIST

D1521369

SUNBURY
P R E S S
Mechanicsburg, PA USA

Published by Sunbury Press, Inc.
Mechanicsburg, Pennsylvania

www.sunburypress.com

For information about special discounts for bulk purchases, please contact Sunbury Press Orders Dept. at (855) 338-8359 or orders@sunburypress.com.

To request one of our authors for speaking engagements or book signings, please contact Sunbury Press Publicity Dept. at publicity@sunburypress.com.

FIRST SUNBURY PRESS EDITION: January 2020

Set in Adobe Garamond | Interior design by Crystal Devine | Cover design by Lawrence Knorr | Edited by Lawrence Knorr.

Publisher's Cataloging-in-Publication Data
Names: Rist, Helga, author
Title: The blood letter: how a young woman survived four soviet east german prisons / Helga Rist.
Description: First trade paperback edition. | Mechanicsburg, PA : Sunbury Press, 2020.
Summary: The memoir of a female survivor of soviet prisons in post-war east germany.
Identifiers: LCCN 2019955156 | ISBN 978-1-620063-41-5 (softcover)
Subjects: BIOGRAPHY & AUTOBIOGRAPHY / Women | BIOGRAPHY & AUTOBIOGRAPHY / Personal Memoirs | HISTORY / Europe / Eastern | HISTORY / Europe / Germany | SOCIAL SCIENCE / Penology | HISTORY / Russia & the Former Soviet Union.

Product of the United States of America
0 1 1 2 3 5 8 13 21 34 55

Continue the Enlightenment!

This book is dedicated to my beloved parents who gave me the most happy, carefree, and loving childhood possible.

CONTENTS

FOREWORD

Sometimes, when I was alone, I felt as if I were surrounded in a thick fog, without the slightest chance of escaping out of it. Hermann Hesse's poem "Im Nebel" entered my mind.

In Deepest Fog

1. Strange to walk in thick fog.
   Lonely is every bush, stone, and rock.
   No tree sees its neighbor;
   Each is alone.

2. Full of friends was my world,
   When my life was in sunshine.
   Now, since the fog engulfs me,
   None are any longer visible.

3. Truly, no one is wise
   Who does not know the darkness,
   Which inescapably and softly
   Separates us from all.

4. Strange to walk in the fog;
   Life is loneliness.
   No man really knows the next one.
   Each is alone.

Translation by Helga E. Rist, 2017

ACKNOWLEDGMENTS

MY HEART-FELT thanks go to Ruth Brommer and Janet Kelley for proofreading and correcting my manuscript. English is not my native language. Thanks, also, to Burke and Barbara McLemore for their advice, counsel, and proofreading.

POTSDAM

YOU HIBERNATED a very long time, my dear diary; since October 14th, 1947, when the darkest day of my life began. I had been in the middle of my *Oberprima* final high school exams (twelfth grade). During the last two weeks, I had written three papers in *Klausur* (in class): a five-hour English paper, a six-hour German paper, and a five-hour Latin paper. The last two remaining exams were a six-hour Mathematics exam and a six-hour Science exam. However, I was no longer in Frankfurt/Oder but had been arrested and detained in Potsdam, a small town near Berlin. I shall now ask my memory to recall as much as possible of all the events that happened during the most horrible eight-and-one-half years of my life.

I had no exam to write on Tuesday, October 14, 1947. Around 7:00 A.M., my parents and I were still asleep when the doorbell rang, and boots pounded against our door. Dad opened it, and when I heard Russian voices, I knew instinctively that the Soviets had come to arrest me. Fourteen persons had been arrested on this day in Frankfurt/Oder by the NKWD (the equivalent of the American FBI): students, teachers, an architect, and a former member of the city council. In the past several months, this had happened to other young adults, including three from my high school class. They all disappeared without a trace. We all assumed that the Soviets used them as slave labor, far away in the Soviet Union, as part of so many war reparations. For example, they had stripped most factories of machines and equipment. They took along the people who knew how to run the machines, but of course, without their families. They ripped and cut up many railroad tracks, then shipped the pieces to the Soviet Union to be melted down. There was only one track left between Frankfurt and Berlin, (eighty kilometers or about sixty miles), and that one train was the only connection between the two cities. Often, this track was needed for a Soviet military train. No problem. The German train was pushed onto a short stretch of the side track and remained there for many hours. We were the last on the priority list! I once had to wait overnight until my train reached East Berlin the next morning. The Soviets forced German engineers to drive hundreds of locomotives through Poland to the Russian border. There the engines sat and rusted because all Russian tracks are much narrower. The German engineers came home. So now, I thought, it was the girls' turn to work as their slaves.

Two Soviet officers and an East German Communist policeman burst into my bedroom and told me (I understood them because all students were forced to take Russian in school, every day) to get up and get dressed, but they remained there in my bedroom. It took my Dad a long time and much skillful persuasion to make them leave my room while I was getting dressed. One of the officers spoke a little German, so my Dad tried to get some information from him about why I was being arrested and where they were taking me. The only answer he received was silence. Mum and I tried as silently as possible to open the window so that I could jump out from the first floor. But who grinned at me standing under my window? A Mongolian soldier who pointed his bayonet right at me. We did not know then that another one like that stood in the back of the house. I got dressed as warmly as I could, then took my watch off, because this was the first thing all Soviets stole from everyone when they invaded the country. But I forgot to take off my snake ring, which I permanently wore. Mum had received it from her godfather for her confirmation. She gave it to me when she was unable to wear it due to arthritic-swollen fingers. I was told to take three blankets and three changes of bed linen. I took one of each because I expected that all would be stolen from me anyway. I also took my toothbrush, a comb, a hairbrush, a cake of soap, and a face cloth. They told me to wrap everything in the blanket instead of taking a suitcase. And then came the moment of goodbye. None of us cried; we were too shocked to cry. I was convinced that I would never, ever see them again. Mum said she agreed: "You will never see me again!" Dad said nothing. We hugged and kissed, but the officers tore me away quickly and pushed me forcefully out of the door. In the entrance hall, I looked around and realized that I had never noticed or realized how beautifully the walls were painted in beige with green and brown colorations. Next thought: I shall never see it again.

The Mongolian from outside my window had informed the officers of my attempt to flee; consequently, from that moment on, all three of them watched me every minute, even on the toilet. Later, I was so very glad that I had been unable to escape. Dieter Zuschneid, a classmate, succeeded in escaping through a cellar window. In turn, the Soviets arrested his mother as a hostage, because Moscow paid them the equivalent of $25.00 or more if the arrest led to a conviction. His father had been killed in battle in Russia. Dieter was able to remain hidden and eventually was able to find a way at night to the border of West Berlin.

It was hard to believe how thoroughly they searched my room and all other rooms as well, turning everything upside down. My bed was emptied down to the metal springs; each picture was taken from the walls. There was not a single drawer in the chest which was not emptied onto the carpet. When they saw photos of Hans Bartel, a friend of my girlfriend Inge and me, as well as a picture of Dieter Linke, the Russians smiled and confiscated both pictures. This gave me the idea that Hans and Dieter must have had something to do with my arrest. Hans and Dieter had disappeared from the surface of the earth in July of 1947. The Russians also took a few booklets of my handwritten diary notes and all of my German movie star pictures, because they had no idea who they were. Much later, I understood why. They expected them to be members of an illegal, underground anti-Soviet Resistance organization. They constantly urged me to hurry up. I put on my warmest clothes: pants, my cranberry pullover, and my thick, blue winter coat, thinking that maybe Siberia was in my future. The most horrible event of my entire life, the moment of goodbye, could not be postponed any longer. I crossed the sunny street and looked back at our house. My heart reached the point of breaking when I saw my beloved parents, their fearful eyes wide open in desperation. Then I saw a classmate of mine, a friend, coming towards me. When he saw me being accompanied by those four Soviets, he looked to the ground and immediately crossed the street. I would have done the same thing. He was the one who informed our class and the school about my arrest. The final Math exam took place the next day, on Wednesday, without me.

I did not cry. I was not afraid. I did not even hate those men who brought this drastic change, which destroyed my life completely. They were nothing but executing peons, tools of the Soviet regime, doing what they were told to do. Their dirty appearance was disgusting though, I was calm, serenely composed. I may have been in shock. It was simply too overwhelming, having had my life broken into pieces. I had no full conception yet about what had happened. I was fully aware that neither my parents nor I could do anything about it, and that I was totally at the mercy of the Soviets. I had no choice at all; I had to do everything the masters demanded. In a way, I was sort of curious about what would happen to me next. We walked along the Gelbe Presse Street, where my closest and most beloved girlfriend, Inge, lived. We felt towards each other more like sisters than friends. There was not a single secret, hobby or interest that we did not share. Since we lived so close, we could spend most of our free time together. Both of our fathers were independent business owners; our parents were friends and Inge and I had shared our lives since Kindergarten. I remember thinking: better I here in this situation than you, but you will still have to write your six-hour Math *Klausur* in class tomorrow. I won't. And you will receive your final diploma and proceed right into a university. My blissful ignorance about her only lasted until the afternoon. She would not be writing the Math exam either.

At 6:00 A.M., she was still in bed and alone at her home. Her parents and sister had pedaled out of town very early in the morning to search for some overlooked potatoes in a field where the potatoes had already been harvested the previous day. (Every single potato was worth a lot for city people at that hungry time.) At her house, the doorbell rang. Inge opened the front door and was shoved aside. Two Soviet officers and a German policeman searched the house, just like it was done at my home. But here they also took a few things which they liked: like jewelry. Inge, as had I, did not even bother to ask questions. But expecting the Soviet Union in her future, she also dressed in her warmest dark blue woolen dress and her winter topcoat. She was not permitted to leave any good-bye note to her family. The Soviets arrested fourteen Germans of all ages on October 14, 1947.

I was taken to the cellar in the GPU Building (GPU was the local Soviet FBI) and locked into an empty cell with a large board to sit on. Inge was already in one of the cellar prison rooms when I arrived. I think my heart skipped a beat when, to my horror, I saw her later emerge from that Soviet building. A few minutes later, boots came down the basement steps, and the name "Stern" was called. This could only be Jochen Stern, a former student at my school. Not knowing that I was not permitted to speak, I called through the closed door, "Sternchen, I am here, also. Helga." The answer was an angry crash against my door and a soldier shouting, "Quiet!" A few minutes later, he opened my door and raised his rifle butt, but he did not hit me. I understood his Russian: "You speak one more word, and I shall kill you!" I was not afraid of this threat because an ordinary soldier would not be permitted to kill me.

During the week before my arrest, Inge and I had studied so hard for the final exams, (which in Germany are the equivalent of American college entrance exams), that we did not get much sleep. It is almost impossible to believe, but I indeed fell asleep in my prison cell. Also, the thought crossed my mind that if I became a slave laborer in the Soviet Union or Siberia, I would probably get a bare minimum of sleep. I woke up when my door opened, and an old man was pushed into my cell with the guard's warning, "Speak not one word!" Mr. Vogel offered me some of his cookies, but I refused to take one. It was much too uncertain if or when we would ever get anything to eat. Later at the trial, I learned that Mr. Vogel had run a Red Cross Shelter in a railroad station. He did not know who slept on his cots for a few hours or a night. But among those who did were several young men, some of whom did some illegal work against the Soviet government while traveling to West Berlin by train. Mr. Vogel's sentence for "supporting illegal actions" was twenty-five years imprisonment. He died of tuberculosis and starvation after two or three years.

According to the moving sun, it was afternoon when all prisoners were ushered to the enclosed courtyard, where two open trucks, each with two benches were waiting. I saw a familiar face, Jochen Stem, and then Inge! What a horrible blow to me! There were many others whom I did not know. We filled the two trucks. She and I were not allowed to sit on the truck next to each other. Even speaking just one word was most strictly forbidden, and indeed, was rewarded with a heavy blow to the head of the offender. Consequently, there was dead silence. Several soldiers with bayonets fastened to their rifles stood between the benches.

To my great and most pleasant surprise, the trucks did not ride towards the east, (i.e., the Soviet Union), but traveled west on the Autobahn to Berlin. They stopped at Frederick the Great's military prison in Potsdam near Berlin on Lindenstrasset. We were stripped naked and then searched, but they overlooked my snake ring. They found my nail file and small scissors in my belongings. Both were thrown into a trash basket. I got dressed and was led by two soldiers through a maze of metal hallways, over countless staircases, passing by cell door after cell door.

In front of each cell sat one or more white porcelain bowls, empty. They do feed people here, I thought, and even in porcelain bowls. I had expected tins in prison. I became the occupant of cell number eighty-one on the fourth floor. Two doors crashed shut behind me; both were locked. The dark green painted cell was about four square meters big, two and a half meters long and one and a half meters wide. A straw sack was lying on the one single, steel frame bed with a few personal belongings on it. Fastened to the wall were a small folding table and a very small folding seat. A small iron-barred window sat high up near the ceiling, but from the outside, there were boards fastened which prevented any view down into the square courtyard, and they also did not allow much daylight get into the cell. In the corner sat a pail with a lid, a "potty."

Sitting there alone, the suppressed tension of my mind released itself, and I started to cry in desperate hopelessness. All of my previous calm composure had vanished. It wasn't long before the doors opened. A friendly, middle-aged lady joined me, named Mrs. Finke from Magdeburg. During the evening, she informed me about many things that a prisoner needs to know. There was, for example, the art of knocking to get in touch with the neighboring cells. Each letter has as many knocks as its place in the alphabet. For example, for the word 'dog' you would use four knocks for the 'd,' then fifteen knocks for the 'o,' then seven knocks for the 'g,' followed by a long scratch, which meant the end of a word. Communication that way takes a lot of time, but that's what prisoners have in abundance.

Mrs. Finke knew all the cases of the neighboring cells, and all of them were ridiculous. Someone criticized the Soviets, an informer heard it; someone dated a Soviet soldier who deserted; someone was falsely accused of spying or being connected in some way to an underground movement. Proof or no proof did not matter; there was no defense or jury at any trial, anyway. Mrs. Finke had been there for a few months, but she had never heard of anyone being released to freedom from this house. She knew that after many cruel, beastly hearings with many beatings, each person came before a Soviet trial, at which almost all prisoners were sentenced to twenty-five years in a hard labor camp. The death sentence, performed immediately after the trial, had been abolished in East Germany just a few months before, in the summer of 1947. However, if execution was the real intention, the prisoners were sent to Moscow, where they would be sentenced to death and executed. After the trials in Potsdam, there always followed a transport, whether to another prison or to the Soviet Union, where the most dangerous offenders against the Soviet Union would end up, thousands of them. My question was, of what would they falsely accuse Inge and me?

The Soviets did not leave me in the dark for long. Already the next day, a guard took me to another part of the prison, to Officer Tobartschikow. I learned that there was supposed to be an underground anti-Soviet organization active in Frankfurt/Oder and a few other small towns, to which about three hundred members allegedly belonged. They supplied the Americans in West Berlin with information which was useful for them. For example, Soviet troop movements could be monitored by using the Soviet truck's license plate numbers. Active members were Hans Bartel, Dieter Zuschneid, and Klaus and Werner Niepmann from my high school class. But they talked to no outsiders about it, because it was much too dangerous! I did not believe Officer Tobartschikow when he and his Russian translator, a very cruel, sadistic woman, told me that Hans had confessed the following: He had told Inge and me about the organization, recruited us, and we agreed to join. Hours and hours filled with the same questions followed: Who are your friends? Who belonged to the organization? Where did you meet? I always denied everything. This scene repeated itself for several months. He hit me a few times, but only with his hand. But the female Satan, his translator, hit me at most sessions, sometimes in my face with her ruler. Once she hit my head so hard with her hand that I almost fell off my chair, which had no back.

Another day when she was standing next to me with a fireplace poker in her hand asking me a question which I definitely would answer with "no," I bent my head and protected it with my arms. I was afraid that she might break my nose, cut off one of my ears or punch one of my eyes out of its socket. Then I mumbled "no." she hit my shoulder with the poker but broke no bone.

I knew but never admitted, that Hans had torn Soviet propaganda papers from walls, and that he, like all of us, would have loved to have gotten rid of these uncultured, dirty invaders, who treated all Germans as despicable, disposable trash. I knew but never admitted, that Hans sometimes pulled out his little notebook and wrote something down, which he never let us read. He said it was something very personal. He sometimes took the train to Berlin "to visit his aunt" he said. But I knew nothing about a spy organization with weapons, munition, and sabotage plans. Much later, I found out that all of this existed. But even if I had known, I would never have agreed to become a member, mainly not to endanger my parents. My patriotism was never stronger than my family ties. And also, such trivial information was not worth the enormous risk.

When I persistently and doggedly continued to refuse to admit to anything that they accused me of, Officer Tobartschikow ordered *Karzer* for me. *Karzer* was an empty cell, divided horizontally into two sections by a screened wall. Thick iron bars were cemented solidly into both walls and the floor and ceiling. There was a door in this partition. There was a small window wide open, high up near the ceiling, with bars.

I had to undress, but Officer Tobartschikow had given instructions that I was allowed to keep my bra and panties on, which was rare in *Karzer*. I was pushed into the part of the room farthest from the door. Two guards looked at me, grinned, and left. I was no beauty, only skin and bones because our food consisted of one piece of bread, about two-and-one-half inches thick, two cups of sweet black coffee, and one bowl of greasy hot water per day. If I was lucky, I had half a piece of potato or half of a carrot or a cabbage leaf in my soup, but nothing else, ever. The guards were not interested in looking at me. They saw the same

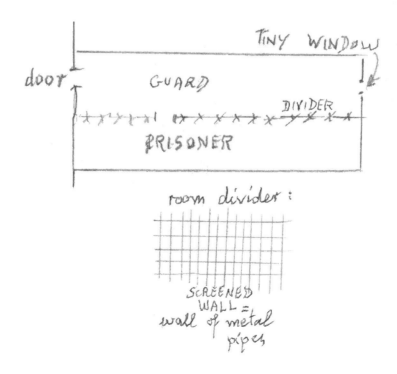

thing every day. To my great relief, Officer Tobartschikow had ordered the guard not to turn on the ice-cold water and point the hose at me, as was done frequently. It was January and the cold wind blowing in through the open window made me freeze anyway, being half-naked. I decided to use the bars for some simple calisthenics. I gripped a bar above my head, pulled up, and did a few knee bends. After a little while, my blood circulated better, and I was no longer freezing quite as badly. But unfortunately, I did not hear the guard approaching. He yelled at me, pointed at my bra and panties, and told me he would take those away if I did not stand still between the wall and the bars. I looked at him most frightened, but this did not stop me from doing my exercises after he had left. From then on, I just listened more attentively for the faintest sound of boot steps. It worked. I do not know how long I stayed in the *Karzer* cell, maybe three or four hours. I guessed by watching a tiny sun ray move, high up on the dark green wall. It managed to squeeze through the wooden shutters outside the window. I loved this little loyal friend that kept me company and talked to me. It said, "Look, watch me move out of here! You will do the same, trust me!" It could not warm up the subzero temperature (Celsius), but it did warm up my heart. After I finally was allowed to put my clothes on, I was taken immediately to Officer Tobartschikow's office. He asked me again and again to admit my involvement in the underground movement and to sign a paper with that statement. The beastly interpreter, a Soviet woman, threatened me with water *Karzer* the next time, but I continued to refuse to admit to anything false.

Wise Mrs. Finke was of a different opinion. She told me again that nobody had ever left this house alive, and that the Soviets would eventually sign the paper of admissions themselves. No one would listen to my objections. I would get a trial, get a sentence of twenty-five years like everybody else, and then finally be shipped out to another prison or to the Soviet Union to serve my sentence. If I stubbornly refused to admit, she said, I would surely get water *Karzer* and less food. My health, maybe my life, would be endangered, without changing the result. If I signed the paper, there would be no more hearings, no more beatings;

they would leave me alone, and I would stew in a cell, waiting for my trial. Mrs. Finke was correct in everything, but I was not willing to do it.

Like most children enjoy making noise, so did the guards. While walking or running, they let their large keys bang at each vertical bar of the long railings, which caused a terrible noise. But on the other hand, they sometimes sneaked as silently as a cat along the metal gangway. And just as silently, pushed the flap over the peephole a little aside to see if we were doing anything forbidden, like sleeping, and then surprise the unsuspecting offender with a hard blow to the body or head. When I could not keep my eyes open after having spent half the night in hearings, I sat on the bed with my head turned to the window, eyes closed.

In the very beginning of my incarceration, I was anxious to give my parents a sign that I was in Potsdam, not in the Soviet Union, but how? Once in a great while, a guard brought a Soviet nurse to the door of each cell. She had no medicines at all, but she had Vaseline, which she smeared on a piece of paper and gave us if needed. Paper was the first thing I needed for a note to my parents. So, I asked for Vaseline and got it. Luckily, the Vaseline was smeared only on one corner of the paper so that I could tear it off and have a small non-greasy piece left. But what about pen and ink? How to get them? I had an idea. Ink was easy to get because Mrs. Finke had a needle which was overlooked when her clothes were searched at arrest. I intended to prick the tip of the little finger on my left hand and use my blood as ink. To make a pen was not that easy. It had to be a piece of straw from our straw sack. First, I had to find a piece that was not too thick and not too thin. Then I slowly rubbed the end on our concrete floor until it was no longer straight but pointed. The drop of blood lasted only for one or two letters, and I had to prick the finger again. Mrs. Finke and I listened to the very best of our ability to hear any footsteps. If a guard had looked through the peephole in the door and seen me writing and found the needle and paper, we would have been beaten mercilessly and then reported to our respective officers. I have no idea what the "Satan" would have done to me. –Water *Karzer* for sure! But I got away with my "crime." Because of frequent, unexpected searches of all cells, I hid the letter on my body. At that time, at the beginning of my incarceration, I still was naive enough to hope that I might get another cellmate, who might go home. Mrs. Finke insisted, "definitely not." Her husband had found a girlfriend, and they wanted to get married. To get rid of his wife, he told the Soviet GPU (NKWD) that she had spoken again and again against the Soviets. Who did not privately do so? She was eventually sentenced to the customary twenty-five years, but she survived only a few of them, like Mr. Vogel. It was so easy to remove people from society! Rubles rolled for each arrest and conviction!

THE BLOOD LETTER

On the small scrap of greasy paper, here is what I wrote:

My three beloved ones, stay healthy like I am. I am fine. We are in Potsdam for investigation; then, probably will spend some time in a camp. Do not worry about me. It is peaceful and warm here, food good. Mom should see Dr. Vaubel (a famous arthritis doctor) and other doctors. Is Dad home? Do you still have any contact with Gebi (my boyfriend)? Do not leave Mom home alone very much. Give Gebi our emergency address (my Dad's cousin) in West Germany. Did you return the fifty marks to Monika? (I had borrowed it to pay for my private Latin lesson because I had forgotten my billfold.) Did you get my three completed final exam papers from school? (The Soviets had confiscated them.) Dear Daddy, can you help Gebi a little, financially? Be courageous, never give up hope, like I. I am living on hope, memories, and faith that I will come home. We just must wait. Thanks for all your love and having been so very good parents to me, all my life long. Forgive me the worries that I sometimes burdened you with and forget all the bad times. I am here totally innocent. They do not believe me. My loving thoughts are with you always. Mom, Dad, Gebi. Greetings, kisses and all my love, and keep me in your love.
A postscript read: I am still here in Potsdam. Helga
(see photo on page 16)

This letter contained many lies, hoping that I could keep my parents from worrying. There was no peace, but constant harassment, beatings at each interrogation, mistreatment, peephole watching, and this terrible hunger. We were often freezing in our ice-cold cell in midwinter when they turned the heat completely off. Our exercises did not help much. I used many abbreviations in the original German blood letter.

I had asked Officer Tobartschikow, again and again, to let me hear the accusations out of Hans' mouth. It was always denied. Then one day I could hardly believe my luck. He said, "You will get your wish. Hans will tell you himself. He sent me back to my cell, and I dreamed of going home. Mrs. Finke warned me not to be too optimistic. She feared that there might be something fishy about that. She was correct.

The next night, (almost all hearings were held during the night, so that the prisoners were dead tired, having been forced to be up since 4:00 A.M.). Officer Tobartschikow said, "Well, now Hans will tell you." I was so excited I could not sit still. I was convinced he would say "no" to those accusations. The door opened. Major Silvakow, Hans' officer, who had the reputation among the prisoners as "the most brutal and toughest thug," pushed Hans into our room. I barely recognized him. The sight I saw was deeply shocking! Bloody scars covered his shaved head and face. His facial expression revealed the beginning of insanity.

He walked like an older man, bent over and as if in pain. I saw him for a very brief moment only, because Major Silvakow immediately pushed Hans on a chair behind a tall bookcase. We could not see each other. Right away, Silvakow asked him, "Was Helga Wunsch an active member of the underground organization?" Hans answered, "Yes." That same moment Silvakow grabbed his shoulders and pushed his head down so that he was looking at the floor, and shoved him out of the room. It was all over in a matter of one second. I was dumbfounded! I was unable to evaluate what had just happened. The floor seemed to disappear under my feet, and I was sinking into a deep black abyss. Officer Tobartschikow's voice broke my stunned bewilderment. "Will you sign now?" he asked. My vocal cords were paralyzed. I was unable to speak. I only shook my head. He did not expect anything else. He called a guard and sent me back to my cell.

I now realized how futile, senseless, and suicidal it was to continue to refuse to sign the confession. I signed it the next day, and I had no further hearings. All my hope of ever going home had completely vanished. That was the end of the beatings, mistreatment, and fear of water *Karzer* which in other prisoners (maybe Heinz and Hans) often triggered pneumonia and tuberculosis. We were isolated from the free world, which expected us to be in the Soviet Union. Who would know whether or not we left this building dead or alive? Who would know there was no plaintiff, no judge or jury? I was left alone, now, and just had to conquer the fierce hunger. I was so skinny that even my monthly period had stopped. My body knew what to do. It could not spare even one drop of blood. And I had to conquer the depressing boredom. No books or newspapers, no pencil or paper, no needlework, nothing at all to stimulate my mind or creativity between 4 A.M. and 11 P.M. Sleeping was strictly forbidden and enforced regularly, to keep us dead-tired during the nightly investigations. Even conversations with Mrs. Finke were exhausted after a while.

ASIDE: Perhaps it may have been Major Silvakow who was the interrogation officer of Ingeborg Schulze, one of the three sisters from Frankfurt/Oder. Ingeborg's situation must have been one of the worst because one day she was so beaten and mistreated physically and mentally, that she was not able to endure it any longer. (She, too, was threatened with the arrest of her parents.) As soon as the officer left the room for a moment, she ran to the locked window and pushed her weight against it. It broke, and she jumped from the second floor into the cement courtyard, hoping to kill herself. Fortunately, she was unsuccessful and was still alive because she had landed on her buttocks. Her sisters were told that she had been taken to a hospital, which was true. There she was locked into a single room. The German doctors and nurses must have given her outstanding care because when she later rejoined the rest of us in Bautzen, she did not even limp!

Helga at age 3 in 1931.

Helga's room at her parents' house.

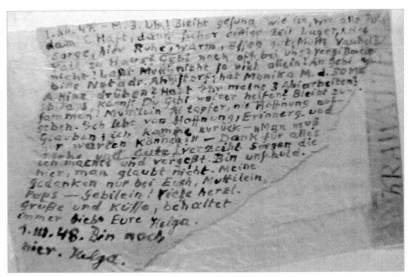

The blood letter.

Helga's parents' house in Frankfurt-Oder. She was arrested here on October 14, 1947.

Helga, one to two weeks before her arrest.

Helga's parents Dora and Kurt Wunsch soon after she was captured.

Helga's parents in the 1950s after they knew their daughter was alive.

Cells inside Potsdam's prison.

Stairs inside Potsdam.

INGE

ONE DAY, I was thrilled and overjoyed when Inge knocked at our wall. Some work had to be done in her cell. It was most lovely to have direct contact with each other, even though we did not expect this to last long. Someone would soon detect that we were of the same case. They did. She told me that she was accused of more than I was, but had also denied everything. Officer Tobartschikow had told me that Inge had admitted everything! She was accused of having reported to Hans that she had seen a train full of Soviet armored tanks, rolling from Poland into East Germany. Such trains did run! This was important military information for West Germany. It was invented, possibly by Hans or maybe by an officer, and Inge had denied it, just like everything else with which Officer Tobartschikow charged her.

Of course, Inge did not tell me about her suicide attempt. She had been alone in her cell, beaten every night by at least the 'Satan,' sometimes by Officer Tobartschikow, like me. She was helpless, hopeless, and in the deepest of depression. She succeeded in pulling a nail out of one shoe and tried to puncture a blue vein in her wrist. Either her hand was not strong enough to puncture the vein, or she lacked enough courage to press hard enough. But one of the guards sneaked with velvet steps from peephole to peephole just at that moment. He confiscated the nail and reported everything to Officer Tobartschikow. The very next day, Inge was moved to another cell with another inmate, Ines. Inge was very lucky to join Ines as they became close friends. Ines was a wonderful lady.

Ines used to live in one of the Baltic states, and like many others, was innocently accused of espionage in prison at Brandenburg. The Brandenburg Military Tribunal sentenced her to death. While she was waiting for her execution, the order from Moscow arrived that all executions in East Germany were to be stopped. Ines was transported from Brandenburg to Potsdam, where there were new interrogations, and she finally received a new sentence. What else? The standard one of twenty-five years.

In Brandenburg, she was forced to watch a pretended execution for no other purpose than to frighten prisoners to death, so that they may admit some new information, true or false. No subhuman treatment was too low, too wretched, too inferior for Stalin's dictatorship.

Inge continued to deny all accusations until the day came when she overheard and understood some of their Russian speech. She heard that they were considering arresting her parents and her sister for questioning. Now she signed all confessions and never had any more interrogation. She permanently stayed with Ines in her cell until our trial.

Many different people crossed the path in my life, but never did I notice, anywhere, such a wonderful, unselfish friendship between any two people as existed between Inge and me. I often realize that, full of gratitude to God! There is, maybe, no better example than a portion out of Harvey Allen's book, *Tonio Adverso* quote:

"A true friendship begins with respect, intensifies to admiration, and ends in unlimited trust, including the first feelings. This process becomes all the more so clearer, the more the friends are willingly ready to offer favors as well as to receive them, without any feeling of obligation or burden on the scale pan of ordinary human vanity, which always desires to be so precisely weighed and measured. True and genuine friendship is high above over this ballgame of obligations, as it is customary in many, selfish, bourgeois acquaintances. A true friendship finds reconciliation because both parts found trust and faith in some eternal blood relation, which connects them. This connection can be reached in quite different fashions, but they are always certain that their fundamental beliefs and actions will meet on a common, eternal foundation."

Up to this day, I have never forgotten to thank God that I was permitted and blessed to have something so utmost powerful and rewarding like my friendship with Inge. How most beautiful and enriching it is to ponder and think alike again, and again, how to come up with countless small joys for such a friend; how to find a way to fulfill small, unspoken wishes of hers, maybe with difficult obstacles in the way. There was simply nothing that occupied our minds, nothing that stirred our emotions in which we were not both deeply interested. It was hard for me to imagine that, in the rest of my life, I would ever again find a person with

Helga and Inge Linke (right) just before their arrest.

whom my thinking and feeling is so much identical, with so few differences. But I was blessed to find her in Camp Hill, in Ruth Brommer. The extent of understanding that she has for me and that I have for her is almost like it was with Inge. How rare in life is something like all this, mutually! It is a very special gift, bestowed on a very few chosen ones. True friendship is the loving and always understanding acceptance of another's uniqueness as well as their shortcomings, never questioning or doubting. A true friend is one who always overlooks your broken fences but admires the flowers in your garden. We like someone "because" but we love someone "although."

HEINZ

ONE DAY, the monotony was broken for a few days. Heinz Blumenstein, a classmate, was put into cell seventy-nine. I had once harbored a crush on him, but he was not interested. Some boy had named him as a friend, and that was always enough for an arrest. He had known nothing about this organization. He also refused to admit to false accusations, and he was in solitary confinement. He told me about Nethe's betrayal, which had started the avalanche of arrests.

Nethe was a member of the organization, and so was another boy who started to date Nethe's girlfriend. In spite of Nethe's threat that he would tell the Soviets about the boy's underground work, he continued to date the girl. Stupid Nethe did not realize that he would incriminate himself, badly. Consequently, he was never permitted by the GPU (Soviet FBI) to leave the GPU building and go home, and he and the other boy were arrested instantly. These were the first two arrests in the spring of 1947.

Now, back to Heinz: Since our two small cells, seventy-nine and eighty-one] were next to the much larger corner cell, eighty, we could talk with each other through open windows if we heard no footsteps of a guard. We also had to listen to the footsteps above us on the roof, where guards walked back and forth. These guards supplied us with a small sense of timing. The sound of the boot steps changed a little after each change of the guards. They could not report us for talking because they

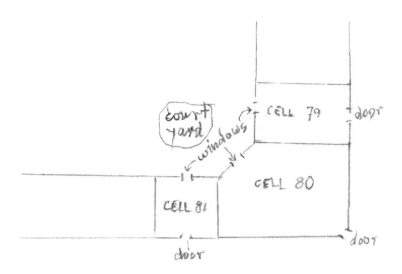

were unable to determine from up there, out of which window the voices came. None of those plain soldiers spoke German.

Heinz told me that his pants were falling because the button tore off. I knew that with a little skill, you could make a needle of sorts out of a strong piece of straw. Heinz did not manage that. So, I made several needles for him. You split the end of a straw with your fingernail, pull a thread out of some piece of clothing, squeeze the thread into the split, and press the straw tightly. You can make only one stitch, then thread your needle again. The other end of your straw-needle had to be rubbed on the concrete floor to get pointed, like making a straw-pen.

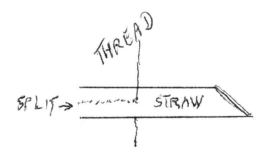

Twice a day, we all had to empty our 'potty' in the toilet cell, then wash our hands and face, one cell at a time. We were not allowed to wash clothes; therefore, my underwear had not been washed for seven months. When the potty-run started at the end of Heinz's gangway, I would follow after him. But whenever the guards decided to start at the other end, I could hide the straw needles somewhere in the toilet cell, and tell Heinz where to find them. Indeed he did, and eventually, he was able to fasten the button to his pants.

Heinz loved to play chess. It was easy to scratch a chessboard into the floor with the end of a spoon, but it took a lot of ingenuity to make thirty-two chess figures out of straw and threads. Since I had no more hearings, I had oceans of time, and I accomplished even that task. I also used a few drops of my blood to distinguish the figures from each other. The king and queen were really cute. A few pieces at a time, Heinz got all of them in the toilet cell. He was so happy! But one day he did not hear the footsteps of a guard, who took all my chess figures, not having the faintest idea of what they were, or what Heinz was doing with them. It was simply intolerable for a prisoner to have a little fun.

Heinz was the best in German in our twelfth-grade class. He was very interested in literature and poetry and wrote poems himself. In his lonesome cell, he composed a love poem for me, a most lovely, tender love poem. The tears poured out of my eyes when I stood by the open window, and he recited this poem to me: How much meaning has one sunbeam on a bright, sunny day? None. But how much does a little bit of warmth on a cold, black winter's night mean? Heinz, it was too late for us, much too late. He starved to death after contracting tuberculosis two years later during November 1949. He was an only child, and all parents in Frankfurt/Oder kept in touch with each other. None of the parents received the remains of their deceased loved ones. They all ended up in mass graves, which were much later discovered around each one of the Soviet incarceration sites. All the families were informed: "Heart Attack, Cremated, Ashes Not Available."

There were frequent strip searches of the cells, and I was scared to death because I had hidden my snake ring under my tongue, in my bra, in my hair, even in my vagina. This day, it was resting in a piece of cotton, (requested for my non-existent period), in the tip of my right boot. The guard examined my clothes, my left boot, and then he reached for the right boot. My heart seemed to be at the point of exploding! But the Lord helped me. The guard grabbed the boot so clumsily that it fell on his toes. He kicked it away angrily, and never touched it again. I could hardly believe my super luck, and I did not even dare to look at my boot with its precious little passenger hidden inside. I did not want to draw the attention of the soldier to this boot, which had not been examined properly. I just said a silent prayer of thanks! This incident made it clear to me that I had to find a permanent, safe place for the ring and the blood letter. I pondered over that for a while, but not long, before I knew the perfect solution. By that time, I had given up any hope for getting my letter out of this building; so, the letter needed a permanent hiding place. The solution for both was my topcoat. I opened the lining and secured my treasures inside of one shoulder pad with a few stitches using Mrs. Finke's needle, then fastened the lining properly. I was sure nobody would find them there. Nobody but my parents ever did find them, but it was many, many years later.

All prisoners knew what date it was because there was not a day that went by when we did not know how many days ago we had been arrested. So, we knew when Christmas was approaching, I could not have asked for a better cellmate than Mrs. Finke, and I wanted to give her a Christmas present. What would make her truly happy? Some extra bread. But it would be too hard for me to have no bread at all myself for one entire day. I started saving a small piece of my ration right away. When I ate the next day, I ate the small piece, and I saved a bigger piece, etc., etc. On Christmas Day, which is December 24 in all German-speaking countries, I handed her an entire day's ration. She was, of course, very happy and so grateful.

Sometimes when going to or coming from an investigation at Officer Tobartschikow's office, I met other prisoners. A few women looked not so skinny, and their clothes were washed and in a little better condition than ours. Our hearing ability had sharpened so amazingly that we were able to distinguish whether a guard's big keys unlocked a cell next door, or two, three or four doors away, or on another floor. Mrs. Finke already knew which cells were frequented regularly. The guards unlocked it, stayed for quite a while, then locked the cell, and continued their peephole walk. We also knew how many soldiers' boot steps it took between cells. The women in those regularly visited cells were not as skinny as we. This was the reason that no guard ever touched us, not even half-naked in *Karzer*.

Shortly after Christmas, another prisoner joined us in cell Eighty-One. I forgot her name; let's call her "Devil" because that's who and what she was. One of us had to sleep on the concrete floor. We took turns. First discovery: she had brought us lice. We sat on the bed for endless days, combing every louse out of our hair, and we indeed succeeded! She had just been arrested for sleeping with a soldier who deserted to the West. She was a prostitute who suffered from all three venereal diseases. Mrs. Finke made her behave, but unfortunately, this did not last long, because, at Mrs. Finke's trial, she was sentenced to the usual twenty-five years and transported away. Never before or after had I wished so desperately to get a cell of my own, solitary confinement. I asked to see Officer Tobartschikow but was ignored. Devil harassed me indescribably for the pure joy of it. When we got a bucket of water to wash the cell floor, I always asked her if she was interested. When she said no, I did it, but then she yelled at me that I, a selfish bastard, begrudged her that little variety during a boring day. When she answered my question with 'yes,' she called me a lousy, stinking idler, too lazy to do a little floor washing. One day I bitterly cried in desperation. In the beginning, when Mrs. Finke was still with us, I was too naive to recognize Devil's abyss-deep, foul character. Unfortunately, I had mentioned my letter and ring in my shoulder pad. Now, Devil wanted to hurt me as hard as she possibly could.

She announced that she was going to tell a guard about my hidden treasures, and she pushed the button, which made a small flag come out of the hallway wall. This was done to speak to a guard. I cried inconsolably; she laughed! God helped me again. The guard was too lazy to push his keys into the door. He pushed the flag back into the wall and walked on. I always let her fetch the two bowls with the hot, greasy water, called soup so that she could keep the one that had a small piece of potato in it. There was no fight, at least, over that.

No words can describe how grateful I was when this cruel torture with Devil came to an end after a few weeks. I was taken out of cell Eighty-One and found a very nice Russian lady in my next cell. Her Soviet husband had deserted, and she had to pay as a hostage before she was able to follow him. She knew she would be shipped to Siberia as similar cases had been.

Utter boredom leads you to the craziest ideas. We knew by wall knocking that in rare, tough, intertwined cases like the Niepmann brothers, who worked actively against the Soviets, it could take a year until the trial, but the average was about six months. I expected this to be Inge's fate and mine as well: we were no "big fish." So, I invented an imaginary clock of twelve hours in my mind. It started running on October 14, 1947, the day of my arrest, and it would be 12:00 around my trial time. If six months equaled twelve hours, one month would be two hours or one hundred twenty minutes. Consequently, my "clock" advanced four minutes each day. Silly, I know. Crazy, I know. It was the brainchild of unlimited boredom.

My imaginary prison-clock reached 12:00 on March 14th, and indeed, two weeks later, our miserable hunger-time in Potsdam approached its end. On March 29th, I was taken to a large room, where all sentencing was done. It was a military courtroom with chairs for thirty prisoners, twenty-two men, and eight women, but we were seven women. (Ingeborg Schulze, who had jumped out of a second-floor window, was still in a hospital. She was sentenced "in absentia"). On the other barrier-separated side of the room, on an elevated platform, sat ten or twelve judges, Soviet officers. No jury. No defense! Soldiers with bayonets on their rifles lined the wall behind us. Inge and I managed to sit next to each other, but it felt like a dagger had pierced my heart when I saw her, skin and bones, like a thirty-year-old woman, grief carved deeply into her beautiful face. I did not know the other five ladies: the two Schulze sisters, Margot, and Gerdi, Anneliese Fricke, Brigitte Grünke and Waltraud Schmidt. I knew Mr. Vogel, Dieter Linke, (later, Inge's husband after amnesty), Sternchen and Hans from the men, but not the twins, Kurt and Eddi Mueller, Rudi Hoffmann, Herbert Zutter, Bernd Becker, Guntram Kohlrusch, Hans Seidel, Nethe or Horst Neumann, or any of the other men. This ridiculous circus lasted for three days and was unsurpassed as mockery. Each person's 'case' was explained in the smallest detail, with an incredible amount of lies. But we were powerless against the bayonets, and strictly forbidden to speak a single word. But Inge and I learned quickly how to communicate. We whispered with almost closed lips! You can do it if you want to. Replace a P or M with sort of a D or G or N, and pronounce all vowels extra-long, and speak very slowly.

After three days, this insane carnival was over. Each prisoner received permission to defend him/herself. Since I knew that this was pointless, I answered "no." Inge did the same as well as almost everybody else. One prisoner said, "I am asking for a longer sentence if my wife is allowed to go home to our children." "Shut up if you have nothing to say about yourself," one of the officers yelled at him. For all of us, the sentence was twenty-five years in hard labor camps, except for Nethe. He got ten years, but he starved to death after two or three years, like Heinz, Hans, and many thousand others. It was important for the Soviet judges to ladle out guilty sentences to as many as possible guilty or innocent Germans because I found out much later they received a lot of reward rubles from Stalin's Moscow headquarters for every conviction. This first sentencing took place on March 31st, 1948, and we giggled that it was nothing but an early April Fool's joke. Two more trials followed after ours. Most of the people had nothing to do with that illegal organization around Frankfurt/Oder. Arrests continued until March of 1948. There was a chain of arrests. They pressed new names out of each new victim. When victims could not possibly be accused of having participated, they were charged with "having known but not reported." ("You must have known because so and so said that he told you").

After the trial, we seven women were taken to my former neighboring cell, cell Eighty (drawing on page 27). I remembered fondly talking to Heinz there, months before. He was not at our trial; neither were the Niepmann brothers, the chiefs of the underground movement, who had

had the most contact with West Berlin and who ended up in Siberia, but both miraculously survived. Those three were sentenced to twenty-five years at a second trial, and even a third one followed with people who had been arrested later.

It was lovely to be together with Inge and the other five, knowing that the hell of Potsdam would soon be behind us if just Siberia were not our next destination. I finally learned many more details about that underground organization, which was no longer confined to Frankfurt/ Oder but had also spread to other small towns. I also learned that one woman was permitted to go home from Potsdam with a threat of life imprisonment if she mentioned Potsdam to anybody, ever! It was the mother of the three Schulze ladies, who then could take care of Margot's infant girl, Barbara, for the following eight years. Mrs. Schulze had been arrested together with her daughters, but she was able to convince the Soviets that she knew nothing about her daughters' doings—collecting license plate numbers of Soviet cars. Of course, the daughters swore to that, also. I am sure that they indeed endangered their parents in no way! It was on April 5th, one day before my most unique birthday, my twentieth, when we all left Potsdam forever. According to our sentences, 'hard labor' was an inescapable threat for all of us. But if the Potsdam starvation had continued, we would have been incapable of hard labor. Consequently, there was hope for more food.

In the inner courtyard, a truck waited for us. Guarded by soldiers, their bayonets in attack position, we were driven to the railroad station. What a marvelous surprise there! The locomotive puffed at the western end of the train. No Siberia! Not even the Soviet Union! It is hard to describe how relieved we were. This was a prison train with steel plates mounted into each window. Tiny holes in the plates allowed a bit of light to get into the compartment so that it was not pitch dark. But much more important was the fact that those tiny holes that we could peep through confirmed to us that we were NOT riding towards the east.

We were able to read the names of some of the towns' stations which we passed. These names indicated that our train was indeed riding towards the west. We had not been informed at the trial where we would serve the twenty-five years of our sentence. We knew that a good number of political prisoners had been transported to the Soviet Union. Many men of the second and third trial of our Frankfurt-case did end up there. Among them were the two brothers, Klaus and Werner Niepmann, the two most active leaders who had started the first contact with West Berlin. Twice the American FBI had sent them home saying: "You are too young. Go back to school." At their third visit, they were told to record Soviet cars' plate numbers secretly. (This informed the Americans about Soviet troop movements.)

Our compartment, which was locked, of course, had two benches of three seats for the ten of us. We squeezed together so that eight of us sat on the benches. The other two (we took turns) could either stand, sit on someone's lap, or sit on the floor. There was no space to move around or exercise. It is really surprising what the human body is capable of tolerating. We vegetated there for three days. We received no food for three days, except for one day. Not because it had just been my twentieth birthday; the soldiers did not know that and would not have cared one bit. Whenever we had to use the train bathroom, we were able to drink train engine water from the little sink. Fortunately, no one got sick from that. There were two Russian ladies with us in the compartment. They had had German friends, which was regarded as patriotic treason. They were sentenced to twenty-five years like almost all of us. We persuaded one of them to go to the toilet. This was only possible when accompanied by a soldier with a pistol in his hand. We wanted her to tell the soldier how terribly, unbearably hungry we were after two days without a morsel of any food and beg him for some. She succeeded and sweet-talked the guard into bringing us an eight-inch plate of plain, cooked macaroni and a small piece of bread with a tablespoon of sugar on it. At first, it was only one good bite of bread and one full spoon of macaroni for each of us. But then, we got a little more from what was left. It was not much for the ten of us, but never did any birthday cake taste more delicious to me!

Heinz Blumenstein died at Bautzen from
starvation and tuberculosis.

BAUTZEN

THIS TWO or three-hour railroad trip from Potsdam to Bautzen took very long because the Soviets had stolen so many railroad tracks all over East Germany. At our destination, we were accompanied by almost as many bayonets and straining, barking dogs as we were in number. We marched, two by two, side by side, through the center of town. All the men were handcuffed to their partner. The main street and all side streets were eerily empty and silent. The Soviets had taken care of that ahead of time. But I saw people standing behind their curtains, and one man raised his arm and waved to us. It seemed obvious to them that we were not criminals, and they also seemed to know our destination, which was a large prison holding 99% political prisoners. My hunger at that moment was not that painful anymore. I was so happy to be out of that awful Potsdam, to be together with Inge and the other friends, and to be still in Germany. I hoped for more food, more than five hours of sleep, more cleanliness—perhaps even a shower, now and then.

My expectations were far surpassed when we entered Building 2 for female prisoners. We were ushered to the second floor, the first being used for something else. Inge and I, pretending we were cousins, together with two other political prisoners, were put into a cell with two sets of bunk beds. Each of us received a bowl for food, and a spoon. Nobody in any cell had to share a bed. Even though always without any meat, the soup was a little thicker and always had potatoes and vegetables. Now and then we got *Nachschlag* (a little more food from leftovers in the large barrels). We also received such luxuries as ten grams of margarine and thirty grams of jam every third day, together with our daily piece of bread, which was about the same size as it had been in Potsdam.

All the administrative duties inside the building were performed by fellow prisoners, even the opening and closing of the cells. To our great joy, all cells remained open during the day, so that we could exchange visits with each other. When we socialized inside, we always found things to do. Someone knew a poem to recite, maybe to memorize; someone told about an interesting book that she had read. We sang folk songs or talked about our families outside. We had fun. We were still hungry, but not as brutally hungry as we had been in Potsdam. We could use the toilets at any time. Our potty in the cell was only for nights.

After the first night, we all broke out in laughter, because each one of us had a new face, so swollen that our eyes were all thin slits: cockroaches in the straw sacks. And they feasted because there had been nobody sleeping on them for days when the house had been prepared for our arrival. All of us had been exhausted after that miserable three-day train trip that none of us awakened during this all-night-long attack.

I, myself, was grateful for the improvements. The interrogations and beatings were gone. I was together with Inge each day. We got a little better food; we got a shower every ten days; we could clean ourselves properly every day in the washroom, we finally were able to wash our underwear whenever necessary, and we were able to use a proper toilet during the day.

How desperately had I longed in Potsdam for fresh air! Now, we were allowed to mingle and socialize for thirty minutes daily, outside. We were watched by soldiers with rifles, but without bayonets. We could not care less. There were always one or two soldiers sitting at the exit door of our building downstairs. They only came upstairs into the large hall with cells for counting heads. Nobody was ever missing; of course, what else?

One day, a perfunctory health exam must have been required. It was given to us by a Soviet doctor or nurse. Every woman, without exception, was declared 'perfectly healthy,' even the women with tuberculosis, which of course, was not treated; yet they remained among us! When I brushed my teeth, a little later, I spit blood, but luckily it did not come from my lungs. It was just periodontis, a shrinking of the gums around the teeth caused by prolonged malnutrition. This lasted for over eight years, finally resulting in the loss of all my teeth. In the doctor's office, there was a mirror on the wall. I could not believe what I saw there. Was I me? This thin face of skin and bones, with abnormally large eyes, set deep in the sockets? It was the face of a forty-year-old woman, and I had just turned twenty! A few of us did not arrive in Bautzen as skinny as the rest of us. They had received extra food from the guards in Potsdam for extra 'favors.' But soon they were just as skinny as we were.

When two soldiers took all of us women to another building for our communal showers, we passed by one of the men's buildings, and I shall never forget the sight at those windows. It was a hospital for men, without any treatment, ever. Ninety-five percent of them had tuberculosis. They were shaved, skeleton-like, wasted skulls with no flesh in their cheeks, and enormously large eyes in deeply sunken eye sockets. All of them were marked by soon-approaching death. They reminded us of pictures we had seen of Nazi concentration camp prisoners, freed after the end of the war. Those faces filled the iron-barred windows behind the glass, one row on top of another. Each one of them tried to get a glimpse of their wife, mother, daughter, or girlfriend. Inge and I were truly glad not to see familiar faces among them.

Heinz and Hans were still alive at that time. All our comrades must have been in different buildings. These buildings for men were larger than our women's building. Those were said to hold over six thousand prisoners. Prisoners did not seem to be moved from one cell to another without any understandable reason to us, like in Potsdam. So, Inge and I hopefully expected that we would stay together in the same cell. We did!

There were different reasons that Inge and I often could stay together in the same cell. Sometimes because of the same age, the same sentence of twenty-five years, the same tribunal, later the same workgroup, and here in Bautzen, it was because fellow prisoners handled all administrative duties. But this changed dramatically later when the Soviets handed over all guard duties to East German Communist policewomen, who maliciously and intentionally separated women who were related or friends. At that time, Inge and I made extra efforts to appear as strangers to them.

Because of the improvements, compared to Potsdam, we hoped that we could remain in Bautzen as long as possible. Unfortunately, it lasted only about three months. At that time, we were told to wrap our few belongings into our blanket. In Bautzen, there were supposed to be men, only.

This transport to a new, unknown location was so horrible; it is really hard to describe. We (about fifty or so women), were stuffed into a cattle car. Two barrels, both rusty, were enthroned in the center of the car. One contained rust-colored water, intended for drinking, which Inge and I never touched throughout three days in a hot midsummer. The other barrel was supposed to be our toilet, which sloshed over the edge after a short time.

There were two platforms at each end of the car, but there was not enough space on them for all of us to lie down. Inge and I were just plain lucky to find room on one of the upper platforms. Some women had to lie on the urine-wet floor at night. Only a few of those had a relative or close friend in the car who would change places with them every second day. Can you blame the rest of us for our survival instinct? We heard the car door locking and a heavy chain being attached from the outside. There were two small windows "decorated" with iron bars and having wooden boards on the outside, preventing almost any view. But there were some tiny holes in the wood boards so that we could read the names of railroad stations which we passed. Those names filled us more and more with horror because they revealed that we were heading east! (Maybe the Soviet Union?) But thank God in Heaven, this was not true. The train stopped outside of Berlin.

We received no food at all during the three days, and the thirst in hot July of 1948 was almost unbearable. The doors and windows were locked shut so that fresh air did not have much of a chance to get into the car, except through small cracks in the walls and the floor. But worse than hunger and thirst for Inge was a mishap which almost broke her heart. At her arrest on that Tuesday morning at her home, she had forgotten to take a silver bracelet off her wrist. She had found all kinds of imaginable hiding places as I had done with my golden snake ring.

But now, locked in the cattle car and safe from Soviet eyes, she had put it on her wrist to feel a little bit comforted by her protecting charm and thoughts of her family. It was no longer on her wrist! The tiny clasp must have opened by itself. We and everybody around us searched and searched, but without any success. It might have fallen on the floor and slipped through a crack. She cried so hard it was heart-breaking for me. At the end of the second day, an old woman died from illness, hunger, and thirst. We carried her to the door and left her lying on the floor until the train had one of its waiting-stops. Then we pounded against the car door and made a terrible noise. Finally, a guard removed the outside chain, unlocked the door, and opened it a few inches. Someone told him in Russian what had happened.

He closed the door and called for a few more guards. They opened the door all the way, screaming at us to get far back from the door, which of course, we did. We moved obediently as we had been thoroughly brain-washed to do. When they saw the dead woman, two of them entered the car, grabbed her by the arms and legs, and with a big swing, tossed her into a grain field outside, where she remained who knows how long!

The door was locked and chained again, but through our little peepholes, we kept seeing the spot where she had fallen like a rock. Nobody came to pick her up during our long waiting time. Then the train moved on.

I heard the characteristic coughing of tuberculosis patients in our car. "But who cared," I thought. It was surprising that more older women did not die during this murderous trip, without any food or drinkable water. Several of them had gray or white hair. It is a marvel, how much a human body is capable of enduring if there is even the smallest glimmer of hope to see one's loved ones outside in freedom again.

SACHSENHAUSEN

ON THE outskirts of Oranienburg, a suburb of Berlin was the former Nazi Concentration Camp "Sachsenhausen" (the houses of the Saxon tribe, 5th century AD). I had no idea that the Soviets, after having freed the Jews and other Nazi prisoners, refilled the camp right away with what they regarded as anti-communist people, mostly Germans. We prisoners were so glad and grateful to still be in Germany and not heading towards one of Stalin's death camps in the Soviet Union, where many millions of innocent victims perished. Stalin even had twenty million of his Soviets killed. Skulls in mass graves, which were unearthed around countless camps, revealed this morbid truth after Stalinism had collapsed. Dictatorships are always ruthlessly cruel, no matter whether Nazis, or the Soviets, or anywhere else in the world. It should be repeatedly pointed out and drummed into the heads and hearts of all the people who are blessed to be free, that freedom is not a gift which falls into somebody's lap. It requires serious and never-ending effort.

"Nobody can, most sincerely, fully and deeply enough comprehend the precious value of freedom, until he/she has lost it. But then you regard it as being sacred." (Heinrich George, one of the greatest German movie stars before and during WWII. George died of starvation in Sachsenhausen Prison, because Hitler had favored him.)

Our train rode inside the camp, and we were finally allowed to disembark. The camp consisted of many battalions. Our battalion, the women's battalion, had eight or ten barracks. Mine was number fifty-eight. Very high wooden fences surrounded the barracks inside of which were layered thick rolls of barbed wire. And inside of that was a live electrical fence. It was virtually impossible to escape from a battalion unless some genius dug a tunnel underground at night. But where would he end up but in the next battalion? A year later, a woman who was unable to bear any more incarceration and separation from her family, waiting until dark, ran to the fence and touched it, instantly electrocuting herself. It flashed through our minds: what an easy, quick, painless death. Who knew what was ahead of us, carrying twenty-five-year sentences? But we all were thinking of our loved ones outside in freedom, who did not even know whether we were dead or alive, whether in Germany or the Soviet Union, and they were worried beyond all imagination. Also, in the farthest back corner of our minds, there still existed a tiny glimmer of hope that someday we would be permitted to breathe the air of freedom again, before our twenty-five years of incarceration were over.

At each corner of our battalion, which was our home for about one and one-half years, Soviet guards watched from small guard posts on stilts. They had loaded rifles pointed at us and big dogs at their sides. Strong floodlights at each tower lit the area like bright sunshine, at night. A few prisoners had already lived in the barracks since 1945, the end of the war. They were either loyal Nazis, who still believed that Hitler was a great hero, or they were innocent women like Mrs. Finke, who had been falsely accused by her communist husband. Many of the women there had had high Nazi positions; all of those had been given "life-long" sentences.

Rows of double bunk beds stretched out on each of the long sides of the barracks. Long wooden tables with benches filled the center of the area. The toilets and the washroom, which had an enormous round basin with many faucets, were located at the end of each barrack. Unfortunately, we were assigned to the barracks alphabetically. This meant that Inge and I were separated because of our family names (Pietsch and Wunsch began with different letters). But this, however, was no tragedy. To our immense joy, we found out that the barracks were never locked. We were not allowed to walk outside of our barracks after dark—the Soviet guards stationed at the exit gate saw to that! But during daylight, we were free to socialize, walk around, visit other barracks, and enjoy fresh air and sunshine as much as we desired inside the triple-layered fence. The fresh air was such a precious gift for all of us! Everyone took daily advantage of that and fully appreciated it. Inge and I spent every day together in her or my barrack or outside, as often as the weather permitted. All comrades shared ideas about little handicraft time-killers, like making little straw dolls as gifts, embroidering doilies, etc. I still have two tiny dolls which Inge had made for me about seventy years ago, and a doily that I had made for Gebi. Of course, many things were made for our beloved family members. They finally received some of those much later, when the German Communist Police forced us to wear prison clothing, and all private clothing and belongings were sent home. That's when my parents found my blood letter and snake ring.

Inge and I did not mind at all that we, "the most dangerous," having sentences of twenty-five years, were not allowed to work, nor were we allowed to leave our battalion at all. However, political inmates with lower sentences, the murderers, thieves, and prostitutes among us were given the privilege of working in the camp kitchen or the laundry. The criminals were even permitted to leave the camp to clean the Soviets' outside apartments and the Soviet administration buildings. It made our mouths water when they talked about the tasty leftovers from the Soviets' meals, which they were permitted to eat.

Once, extra help was needed in the kitchen, and Inge and I volunteered. We had to peel potatoes most of the time and rarely helped to clean vegetables. Raw potatoes taste pretty awful even for a very hungry person, but we did enjoy the rare opportunity to munch on raw vegetables. Even this little kitchen job was exhausting for us in our undernourished condition. So after one week, we did not volunteer again. At a perfunctory, hasty health exam upon our arrival in Sachsenhausen, I found out that I still weighed only eighty-five pounds. Inge weighed about the same. We thought it wiser to relax on our straw sacks or to sit or walk outside of our barracks in the fresh air than to work for nothing. We were never bored.

One day, when we walked from our battalion to the kitchen, we passed by a large smokestack which was no longer in operation. Our Soviet guard asked us, "Do you know what this is?" We did not. Her answer was, "That is where the Nazis incinerated thousands of Jews. But we do not do awful things like that." I thought to myself: you starve people instead.

I knew about the existence of Nazi concentration camps. Everyone learned the unbelievably cruel details after the end of the war. This made me think of my Dad, who, many years ago, had warned me more than once or twice to never mention anything negative about the Nazis in public. It could put the three of us in danger of being sent to a concentration camp. The possibility, even though slight, did exist anyway for this reason. The Nazis did not like our family at all. Neither Dad nor Mom belonged to the Nazi Party, and I did not belong to the Hitler Youth. I had been invited to the meetings, but I realized that it was nothing more than political Nazi brainwashing, and I did not bother attending again.

During the war, a female Hitler Youth Leader, accompanied by a male leader, came to our house. Dad opened the door and told me to come. He asked me in front of them if I would like to go with them. I replied, "No, I do not want to go there again. It's too boring." Then Dad said to them, "It's up to her. I shall not force my daughter!" and he closed our door. Dad did not seem to know any details about the concentration camps. No one did, at that time. For some reason or another, people were afraid to mention those camps. Germans who lived nearby the camps must have noticed that while many transports of people arrived frequently, no one had ever seen anyone come out of the camp. Perhaps those who had worked inside the camps had been sworn to secrecy on penalty of death, so they never mentioned anything outside. Most work had been done there by inmates, anyway. There was no concentration camp near Frankfurt/Oder.

Each morning and evening a loud bell rang for us which meant *Appel,* a roll call inspection by several Soviets. We lined up in rows of ten, side by side. The count was taken, whether in pouring rain or snow. Rarely were the numbers incorrect; the officers were always aware of who was out of the battalion working.

Just like it had been in Bautzen, boredom was kept at bay if one involved herself with activities. There were discussions of books someone had read in freedom, poetry recitations, handcrafting items, storytelling, and philosophical discussions. One lady, a teacher, knew Rainer Maria Rilke's entire lyrical poem, "The Coronet" by heart. A few years later, under different circumstances, Inge and I learned it by memory from her. Both of us tremendously enjoyed reciting with feeling, skill, and intonation, all thirty-four pages whenever one of the other ladies in a dayroom was interested in hearing it.

In Bautzen, we had been tortured each night by bed bugs, living in the straw sacks, which were full of them. That same plague awaited us in Sachsenhausen, but with the addition of jolly and hungry companions, thousands of fleas. They used us for their meals and not just during the nights. Not many complained, though, because we all looked alike, covered with bites. Besides, complaining never helped, anyway, because no one was willing or able to do anything about the situation.

Now and then, searches took place in the barracks, not performed by any Soviet but by women like Mrs. Lambrin, a criminal in our barrack. She searched through all our belongings, looking for something forbidden such as scissors, sewing or knitting needles, a pencil or a knife. But she never found much. When we noticed her starting this dirty job for a little more bread, forbidden things disappeared like magic. Many of us came up with several good ideas for concealing things, which, of course, we shared. She was not allowed to perform body searches, so this was the safest place to hide something. Another good place was the straw sack. I had cut a small opening in the comer of my bag and then pulled a thread out of something. I fastened the thread firmly and permanently to my scissors and small knife. Whenever I noticed her starting a search at one end of the barrack, I pushed my scissors into my straw sack so far that only I could detect the end of the attached thread. It always worked; she never found anything objectionable among my belongings.

Gerdi Schulze, one of the three sisters who had shared our Soviet court trial in Potsdam, was assigned to my barrack. We were about the same age, and we decided to become bunk neighbors. Quite soon, a close friendship grew between us. Gerdi was an angel without any fault or shortcomings. Many a time, I stood outside our barrack, relishing an unbelievably beautiful, colorful, splendid sunset, like I never consciously remember ever seeing before in my life. Or I would gaze at a night sky adorned with a multitude of sparkling stars. They resembled tiny diamonds appliqued onto the dark velvet carpet of glory. The longing for my parents and the resulting homesickness almost tore me apart.

Suddenly Gerdi, or, during the day, Inge, would stand next to me. They said nothing, just putting their hand on my shoulder, as if to say, "You are not alone here; you have sympathetic friends who know what you feel." How comforting for me! And then we would talk about cases much worse than ours. Among us were comrades who left behind very sick loved ones. There were mothers who did not know who cared for their children or whether they had been put into Soviet children's homes with new names so that the mothers would never find them again. This happened. The interrogation officers in Potsdam liked to use such threats to press information out of the despairing mothers. One of our mothers was dragged out of her house, while her small children were playing in the bathtub upstairs. She was not permitted to go upstairs and did not know whether any of the little ones had drowned.

Inge, Gerdi and I comforted and consoled each other, gaining strength from knowing that shared joy is double joy, but shared grief is only half the grief. We pointed out the positives to each other: We were still on German soil, and the chances for getting sent to the Soviet Union were very small now. We noticed that this happened only to Soviet citizens. None of us from Frankfurt/Oder was really, seriously ill. Gerdi's sister, Ingeborg, had miraculously survived her desperate jump out of a second-story window onto a paved courtyard in Potsdam's interrogation prison. She was among us again, without any obvious bad aftereffects, as it seemed. If that was not a miracle, I don't know what one is.

Gerdi and I saved equally from our food rations when we intended to make a cake for special occasion like a birthday. Of course, we could not bake, but we made cold cakes and decorated them beautifully. You can make a cold cake by soaking bread in a tiny amount of water, just enough that you can shape this 'dough' into a round or square form. You slice the dough into two halves with a strong thread, spread margarine, sugar, and jam on the lower half, and then add the upper half. Done is your cake, except for the decorations, which I much enjoyed doing, thanks to a few artistic genes from my Dad. Those 'cakes' tasted delicious to us. We savored them!! I was proud when other women in our barrack asked me to decorate their cake. Inge got an especially beautiful one for her twenty-first birthday on September 2nd. She was so popular and loved by everyone! She received a lot of little gifts for her birthday: a small piece of bread, a little container with jam, small dolls made of straw and colorful yarn, which had been pulled out of pieces of our clothes. Gerdi and I made the cake, arranged a birthday party for her, and made a few other gifts.

Sonia von Rahden, a Russian lady, had a beautiful, warm, well-trained alto voice, and she was experienced in leading a chorus. Inge and I had always sung in school. Consequently, we derived great pleasure out of singing with Sonia's small chorus, usually outside. We also relished the solos with which she sometimes treated us. Even the guards came to listen, now and then.

Outside, in the free world, the green leaves on trees probably changed their outfits to yellow and gold because the autumn had told the summer to move on. The cool nights were anything but enjoyable. I had only the one blanket that I had brought from home. Even my topcoat on top of the blanket did not help much. Finally, some relief arrived. We happily greeted two new additions in each barrack: friendly pot-belly stoves and stacks of firewood. We could toast slices of bread now (how delicious!), not seen for years. We could dry our laundry and our hair much more quickly. In our cozy, warm barrack, I even felt a little sorry for the guards in the watchtowers. We noticed them hitting their arms around their shoulders in this really cold winter and especially during snowstorms.

For a limited time each morning, we received a big knife to cut the large loaves of bread into rations. I was selected to be a bread cutter for a long time, maybe because I can be very accurate. When I was finished, skillful hands carved knitting needles and crochet hooks from suitable pieces of our firewood. I got those very cheaply since I was the one who had the knife!

My new knitting needles gave me a new idea! I had worn my cranberry-red pullover every single day since I had left my parent's home, except for hot summer days. At certain spots, it was thin as a spider web. I told Inge, "I shall re-knit my pullover."

"Where do you think you can get yarn?" she answered. I explained to her that I planned to unravel my pullover, paying very close attention to how it had been knit. I never in my life had knit a pullover, and I shall reinforce the red yarn with threads pulled out of straw sacks, which I shall barter for with some of my cigarettes. You could get all kinds of things for cigarettes. I am not sure why they supplied regular rations of those in Sachsenhausen. Maybe they hoped to increase tuberculosis and get rid of us, or maybe because the Soviets smoked so much themselves. Inge, Gerdi and I did not smoke, so we had nice extra cash! Inge had doubts that this pullover idea would work, but I was pretty confident. I also intended to consult experienced knitters for advice. Indeed, I managed to create a thick, long-sleeved new pullover, lovingly warming me all winter long! But my parents did not recognize it when our personal belongings were sent home later. Besides reknitting my pullover, I found nice, suitable material to make an undershirt and blouse, but not for myself, for my Mom. Addicted smokers sold half their belongings for cigarettes. When these things arrived at home later, they did not fit Mom at all. She no longer had such a slim, schoolgirl figure as she did in 1947. But she valued my loving thought, and it was an enormous joy for me to make them.

Pieces of underwear were unraveled or taken apart by other comrades for the same reason. Many cute little things were created from straw with colorful pieces of cloth. Someone else was busy constructing a deck of very small cards, made of some extra strong paper smuggled in by workers. I had a deck. There was a woman among us who knew Skat. She was willing to teach any of us who were interested. Skat is a popular card game for men, and there are as many Skat Clubs in Germany as Bridge Clubs in the U.S. Dad belonged to one. I also made some straw dolls for others in the barrack, and I embroidered the initials of their mothers, fathers, or whatever family member my comrades were longing for, onto their tiny skirts or pants. The dolls that I received myself had not the faintest idea that they would eventually emigrate to the U.S. I still have them.

The first snowflakes came sailing down, and soon Inge, Gerdi and I had to stomp through a carpet of snow on our daily walks to fill our lungs with fresh air. Christmas was approaching, and almost everyone wanted to give some Christmas present to close friends. Comrades came up with interesting new ideas, which others copied. Gerdi had to come up with more ideas than Inge and I because she had two sisters plus two close friends there. Those Christmas preparations distracted (for a short time) our so very painful memories of former Christmases at home together with our loved ones.

Much baking was going on shortly before Christmas, especially on December 24th, the German main Christmas Day. (December 25th and December 26th are also legal Christmas Holidays, and all offices, as well as many stores, are closed in Germans speaking countries.) Groups of friends sat together in all barracks, exchanging gifts, enjoying the cakes and talking about Christmas at home. Of course, it was impossible to get a Christmas tree or even a few pine branches, but everyone seemed to take that in stride.

Gerdi and I owned many forbidden things, like a knife, scissors, a pencil, even a little mirror, bartered for cigarettes. All prisoners who left our battalion for work went through a required, superficial search. But they were clever enough to hide whatever they wanted to bring into our battalion. That's how all those things were available for us. These workers were not body-searched naked like we all were before every big transport to a new location.

Just like the unstoppable wheel of time constantly rolls one, the snow melted eventually, and it became warmer. Old winter had no choice but had to retreat from the new, young spring, galloping in on a lively, chestnut mare. At the end of March, to our great surprise, the bell rang in midday for *Appell*. Several Soviet officers showed up, which was very unusual. A translator repeated their words: "All of you shall be allowed to write to your family." You would expect that such news would cause an eruption of greatest joy. But our reaction was amazing: dead silence — not a single sign of joy or happiness.

Finally, a short, contemptuous laugh, and another one, and another one. We all laughed at the officers, at this joke which they played on us for their amusement, or so we thought. Nobody believed them. The mistrust against everything that came from Soviet Headquarters was so thoroughly ingrained in us that it seemed simply unthinkable that anything good for us could ever come from them. This was the fruit of all their treatments so far. Most of us could not imagine or believe in any human kindness from them regarding us. Finally, someone yelled, "What a big lie!" Now the officers may have guessed that we did not believe them. They shook their heads, not quite comprehending, turned around and left because they knew that it was true. Many Soviets were not bad or mean, but rules and orders from Moscow could never be trusted; they had always been against us. They had constantly treated us with contemptuous hatred, right from the first day of our arrest.

Shortly after that, I had my twenty-first birthday. So often in my life, this seemed not to be an ordinary day. One year before, we suffered through that three-day transport from Potsdam to Bautzen, without any food. This year, the potbelly stoves were just removed from all barracks, and it was very cold. A fairly large group of us were sitting at my birthday party, dressed in topcoats, gloves, and scarves wrapped around our heads, eating the birthday cake which Inge and Gerdi had made for me.

A few days later, on April 21, 1949, a scream of joy filled our battalion: Postcards and pencils were smiling at us and were quickly distributed. The only women who were not permitted to write were the 'interned' women, former high-ranking Nazis. We were told that we could write to any family member or friend and that we were allowed to receive unlimited answers. We were forbidden to mention anything about Sachsenhausen or anything at all about our former incarceration, which was understandable. But some doubts grew among us. Was this indeed a generous act of humanity in Moscow, something utterly unusual? Or did they want to find out what we thought and how we felt? Did they want to try to trap us? If one of us was careless and expressed a thought against the Soviets or communism, she could be given a new trial and additional years. Not many of us believed that our postcards would be sent home, especially when no mail arrived for several weeks.

However, deep within me, a small spark of hope remained glowing; how could it not? The prospect of their offer was so unimaginably fantastic. But, if true, what would I find out? Would I learn that my parents were still alive? Dad's health was always excellent, but this was not the case with Mom. Her last words tortured my mind: "You shall not see me again. I cannot survive that!" What would her condition be now? And how about other relatives and friends? Was another one of my classmates arrested by the Soviets, without reason or cause? A thousand worries, which seemed common to most of us. But I pushed all doubts aside and concentrated on the thought of how much joy my card could bring to my parents, if, by a miracle, they indeed would get it. I sharpened my pencil so that I was able to write the smallest possible letters, and enjoyed the feeling that at least my thoughts were especially close to them. Finally, the day came when the barrack resounded from another loud shout of overwhelming joy: large boxes of mail were brought into our battalion, mail from the outside, from our loved ones. My mouth popped open in disbelief. Was this true? Inge's and my name were called. We had each received a letter. My heart beat like an alarm clock. I lack the words to describe the wave of emotion that rolled over me when I held the envelope with Dad's dear, familiar, energetic handwriting. I staggered to my barrack, clutching his letter in my hand. I sat down on an outside bench, but I was still unable to pull the letter out. My hands were shaking, and tears swelled into my eyes. All envelopes arrived opened from the censorship where all correspondence was strictly read, and at times, portions cut or blackened out. I finally collected enough courage to pull out the letter.

Nothing was cut or blackened out, but Mom's handwriting was missing. My Dad, himself, had held this piece of paper in his hands. He at least was alive and at home. A flood of passionate love for him filled my heart. I heard sobbing and saw tears flowing when someone had to face bad news, such as a death in the family or the remarriage of a spouse to another person. It was the easiest thing in the world, at that time, to get a divorce if a spouse was sentenced for some political reason. Thank God, no bad news for me. Mom was also alive. She had just spent a few weeks at a health spa to find some relief from her arthritis pain. No cortisone was available at that time. Dad had called her at once, to share the wonderful news that I was alive.

This was the most wonderful, most loving, most profound letter that I had ever received in my entire life, so full of grateful joy. I wish I still had a copy of it. No one was allowed to keep any mail before our next transport. All of my relatives were well. No one else had been arrested according to Dad's knowledge. Dad wrote a note on his calendar May 18, 1949: "Blessed and never forgotten be this day which brought us the great news that our child is alive, after one year and seven months of uncertainty." He framed it, and I do still have this calendar page. Dad also enclosed two small photos of himself and Mom. That indicated that we were also permitted to receive pictures. How they looked like worry and grief had aged them both by many years! I kissed the pictures and the letter. How deeply I loved both of them.

Now, Dad tried relentlessly, begging the Soviet authorities to release me on 'house arrest,' promising that he would never give me any chance to leave the house. He even had his pleas for mercy translated into Russian and mailed them to Moscow. I later read copies of his countless attempts, which no doubt all sailed straight into some waste paper basket. Of course, he never, ever received any response. A little later, we were allowed to write again, this time a fifteen line letter. It was true. We were all permitted to receive unlimited mail and pictures. I don't think there was ever any mail delivery when my name was not called, because not only did my parents write regularly and frequently, but my relatives and friends, former classmates, and even my Latin teacher, Dr. Hutloff and his wife. I still have some photocopies of some of the mail written to me.

Gerda "Gerdi" Schulze died at Hoheneck when she and others succumbed from the effects of poisoned paint.

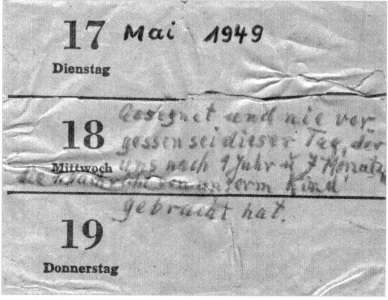

Helga's father's calendar entry for May 18, 1949: "Blessed and never forgotten be this day on which after one year and seven months we got news our daughter is still alive."

GEBI

I HAD DATED a classmate of mine in 1947. His name was Günter Gebauer, but everyone, including his parents, called him Gebi. He was six feet tall, with wavy blonde hair. My parents mentioned in their mail that he did not believe in my sentence of twenty-five years. He believed in an amnesty and was determined to wait for my return and marry me. Inge and I did not believe in an amnesty from the Communists, but from then on, I wrote two or three lines to him in the letters home. He sent me at least one or two long letters each week.

Whenever he came from Rostock, where he was studying, visiting his parents in Frankfurt/Oder, he also visited my parents, and sometimes he even stayed overnight with them. After two years, he asked their permission to call them 'Mom' and 'Dad.' He bought them gifts for birthdays and Christmases. Dad had leased an acre of land, outside of the city limits, to grow potatoes and vegetables himself. I received photos showing Gebi helping him on the plot. All photos and mail were destroyed before our next transport in February 1950.

My parents urged him to date other girls because he had never before had a girlfriend. He did but to no avail. He could not wait to tell them about all their shortcomings, and never dated them again. He had made up his mind!

His special interest and ability were in mathematics. He studied and graduated at the University of Rostock. He was so advanced in math and science that he had taught our senior high school class in 1946 when schools finally opened fifteen months after the end of the war. Two main reasons account for the long delay: (1) Many schools lay in rubble and (2) no teachers could be found. They were either killed in battle or had moved to West Germany, never returning to the Soviet Zone.

Gebi had enriched my life, motivating and stimulating my mind tremendously in Sachsenhausen with his regular supply of a sort-of cor-respondence course in advanced math plus much personal mail. Now, he got good grades in his university classes. He was serious in his intention to wait for my return, even though he knew my sentence. He, like Dad, wrote countless appeals for the return of his fiancée to her home under 'house arrest.' Never any response! The East German Communist officers to whom Dad and Gebi sent their pleas for clemency did not have the tiniest bit of influence on any of our fates. Those were decided not even in the main office in East Berlin, but only in Moscow. Gebi, like Dad, had his pleas translated into Russian and sent them directly to Moscow. No response, of course. Gebi tried hard to stimulate me intellectually with trigonometry, calculus, and integral math assignments. I finally started to remember what I had learned in school but forgotten, having had no books at all. Inge, Gerdi and I spent many hours on Gebi's lectures and assignments, having a wonderful time. He sent us the answers to his assignments a week or so later.

When we were permitted to write a second, fifteen line letter, after three months, I used several lines to ask Gebi to find someone else and forget me. I felt so guilty that he might waste many years of his life without a partner. There was not the slightest glimmer of hope that I or anyone else with a twenty-five-year sentence could be amnestied, as alleged 'spies.' His answer: He just laughed at my suggestion and insisted that no one and nothing could change his mind and intention to wait for me. I received over sixty letters from him in Sachsenhausen. How deeply grateful I was to him for all his many, continuous efforts.

Guenter "Gebi" Gebauer (circa 1947) who waited for Helga
while she was in prison.

A BRIEF RETROSPECT OF THE HORRORS OF POST-WAR GERMANY

We had no idea, at that time, after the end of the war, whether Dad, having been in the Army, was still alive or had been killed. No communication whatsoever was possible in the war-torn country neither by writing nor by telephone. Every German received a ration card from the Soviets, which allowed us to buy one two-pound loaf of bread and one cup of jam per week. That was all, no exceptions. There was nothing else in the few bakeries, anyway. All the shelves were empty. There was no milk for children or babies, nothing extra for the sick or expectant mothers. So many people in Frankfurt/Oder starved daily, ending up in mass graves without coffins or identification.

Dysentery and typhoid spread like wildfire. Grandmother, Mom, and I were not spared, but we survived somehow, even without any medication. The Lord did not want us to die at that time. Since most schools were closed or destroyed, seven of them were used as extra hospitals.

For several months, we had no utility services at all. Tap water was returned first because the Soviets needed it badly. Mom knew a spot where Mother Earth gave us the present of a small spring whose cold water trickled out from between a crack in the rocks. We had clean drinking water, but the dishes remained unwashed. There were no showers or baths.

In Frankfurt, every single shop and store closed after the war. The Soviets had confiscated everything inside. Whatever they did not need right then and there, was packed by German slaves and sent to the Soviet Union. Mom and I ate acacia blossoms, baby dandelion leaves, wild mushrooms, berries, and herbs. We sneaked into fields at night to steal a few potatoes or vegetables. Then we left money in the farmer's mailboxes. The farmers who saw Germans taking some potatoes or vegetables from their fields looked the other way. They had seen it happen that some neighboring farmer had been shot when he gave or sold some food to Germans. This was strictly forbidden and enforced. All food produced was only to be used by the Soviet Armed Forces. Especially valuable to them were potatoes, needed for producing their vodka! But such little extra food like Mom and I ate did not help to keep Granny alive. She had just reached her 70th birthday. I visited her as often as I could, in a hospital on the other side of Frankfurt. But on November 8th, her bed was empty. I wanted to bring her a little extra food, but I came too late. The ladies in her room appreciated the food.

They told me, not knowing my name, that Granny's last words had been "Give my love to my most beloved Helga." They also told me that she had received an injection before her passing. My parents and I speculated that this might have been a mercy killing. The fluid in her body had increased and spread so that her thighs had the circumference of my waist. The fluid, a decades-old problem of hers, could have reached her heart, but why the injection?

The hospital had absolutely no medication or treatment like she had had regularly for many years before.

There was no public transportation, no bus, no streetcar, but I had made it safely, walking three hours to the hospital, alone, while the Soviets staggered drunk through the streets, celebrating a three-day patriotic holiday. Of course, I made sure that I did not look my age or attractive in any way. On the way home, her loss sank into me, because she had been the most beloved person in the world for me. But my emotions were also overwhelmed by envy. Granny did not have to suffer any longer.

But for the rest of us, life offered pretty little else but worries, hunger, insecurities, uncertainties, and a desperate struggle to survive. However, we never forgot for a moment to be desperately grateful for Dad's safe homecoming. How often did one of us say, "All three of us!"

Dad did get a coffin for my grandmother. He had returned safe and sound from the army, thank God, after hiding in the Alps on a high mountain during the last days of fighting. Kind Alpine village people provided him with food and civilian clothing. Dad knew a carpenter in Frankfurt from whom he could barter a coffin for some of our belongings. Granny had a proper funeral and was buried in our family plot.

It was a big birthday present for me when my paternal grandmother gave me a piece of bread, the size of four fingers, and one egg for my seventeenth birthday. She asked me how I would like to have the egg prepared. I chose fried, sunny-side up. This was like a gourmet meal! My grandparents used almost all of the eggs of their chickens for bartering.

They had refused to evacuate when the Soviet armies approached. I guess my grandfather, the owner of a small neighborhood bakery, expected that the Soviets would need him for providing bread for their armed forces and that they would supply him with flour to do that, i.e., they would have bread themselves to eat. He was right. However, before this could be arranged, his wife and daughter-in-law had to be protected from the Soviets' propensity for raping every female they could find, regardless of age. Grandpa cleaned out his large baker's oven, and the women lived in the back of it. He put stuff in front of them so that nobody could see them, and they only came out late at night. It worked like a charm! When he then started baking bread for the Soviets, he was sort of like an employee of the Soviets, and no one would ever bother grandma and my aunt.

He was strictly forbidden to sell or give any bread to Germans, unless for their rationing cards. He had to obey because the Soviets encouraged or bribed more and more Germans to become informers. Soviets were like Nazis. Life was not exactly like a joyous celebration. But I learned from my clever and always optimistic Dad that if circumstances hand you nothing but a sour lemon, it may make life a little easier to bear by thinking of a delicious piece of lemon cake. So, I often try to practice this valuable advice.

The Soviet troops had advanced to the broad, wide Oder River in February of 1945, but did not seem to have any immediate intention to cross it. Mom and I secretly sneaked back into Frankfurt seven times between February and April, from our evacuation town west of Berlin, Rathenow, to fetch more of our household items, including our beloved big Mende radio, wrapped in a feather bed, snoozing in our largest laundry basket. There was always shooting along the river, either from the Soviets on the east shore or from the Germans on the other side. Thirteen-year-old boys and seventy-year-old men were forced by German officers, at gunpoint, to defend western Frankfurt. Many were killed during those last days. When the Soviets were finally given orders to cross the river, they started with burning down most of the inner city. Almost all civilians had been evacuated or had fled except my grandparents, who were living at the outskirts of the city. Consequently, no one was there to fight the fire.

After this flash-back to the after-war horrors of 1945, my dear diary, let us return to Sachsenhausen, in 1949. This portion of my incarceration was pretty good to me; certainly the easiest of all to tolerate. I was blessed with the most wonderful gifts: I still had both of my parents not only alive but in relatively good health, nothing seriously or fatally wrong, anyway. I had two, caring, exceptional friends. Gebi was still waiting for me. I was the proud owner of so many photos. There would never again be any cruel Soviets' interrogation. I really had little to complain about— besides hunger—compared to many others. Mom's doctors had found a more effective treatment against her arthritis. Dad had a successful new business start after his previous one in the downtown center was totally destroyed. Showers of firebombs had burned down ninety-five percent of Frankfurt Town Center.

In Sachsenhausen, I wanted to be able to see my dearly beloved pictures whenever I woke up in the morning or any time that I spent on my bed. A shelf at the foot end was needed for that. I pulled out one of the wooden boards from underneath my straw sack and pushed the remaining boards a little, no problem. I braided straw sack threads into thin but sturdy ropes, which tied the board to the foot end of my bed. But before that, I had covered the board with a colorful piece of cloth, bartered for cigarettes. It was really pretty! I received compliments from comrades, and many were envious of my many pictures. Someone copied my idea, but mine was not only prettier but displayed more pictures than anyone else's. How I did love them!

How much did I cherish the photo of the lily-of-the-valley incline in our back yard, which was covered with a snow-white blanket in spring, and our cozy corner under a lilac roof, where we enjoyed so many a meal. It was the greatest of pleasure to me when comrades admired my wealth of pictures, and I could tell the stories behind them. For a few cigarettes, I was able to find some clear cellophane to protect my photos a bit against the dust, which was a great nuisance when our barrack was cleaned in the morning, and one hundred fifty straw sacks were shaken.

I framed the photos with the cardboard and made little stands for them. No one had any glue, but it is easy to attach papers or cardboard with a few stitches. The plastic traveled from the x-ray department of our battalion hospital into the barracks. My dearest parents did not overlook my desperate longing for photos. How else could I better understand what was going on outside, following their lives and how they were occupying themselves? They also included pictures of the rooms at home and of our garden, and the details inflamed the loveliest memories in me. My room was unchanged, and Mom lovingly watered the big potted palm in the corner next to my large window (see photo on page 15). Almost all of the ordinary windows are larger in Germany than here to let more sunshine get into the rooms. Rarely did the sun get too hot in eastern and northern Germany; therefore, no one had any sunshades at windows. We are on the latitude of central Canada, but the Gulf Stream makes it much warmer.

There were two cups more soup for those who volunteered for *Stubendienst*, barracks cleaning. Gerdi and I did it for a little while, but not long. In our condition of dystrophy, that little extra soup was not worth the physical effort; besides, we were exhausted afterward.

In the Fall of 1949, I started to get an unpleasant and annoying but not dangerous or life-threatening skin problem, caused by the years of long-lasting undernourishment scrofula and furunculous started lightly, but slowly progressed to the formation of fistulous openings. I jumped high with joy when a nurse signed an order to admit me to the battalion hospital because the number of those openings on my body had reached thirty-two. It was well known that the conditions in the hospital barrack were better than those in the rest of the battalion, but when I got there, I could hardly believe what I saw. The straw sacks were much thicker and not filled with just chaff. The German doctors and nurses, all prisoners sentenced for political reasons, were always kind, and best of all, the food was better. Still no meat or luxuries, but thicker soup and more of it. This hospital barrack was part of our battalion, but obviously, we were not allowed to leave it. However, I could snitch a piece of paper, now and then, to communicate with Inge and Gerdi. Once in a while, a Soviet officer showed up, to control the appearance of the hospital and the condition of the patients.

The doctor ordered a cream to be spread on my sores, and a nurse bandaged my arms, legs, and torso. I was told that it would probably take two or three weeks for all those sores to heal. Immediately, the idea crossed my mind: How can I extend this? I found a way! When my sores began to heal, I rubbed them with my dirty blanket. I was aware that this was dangerous, but it worked for about three months without bad consequences. The Lord had decided not to let me die, yet, of blood poisoning. I am sure, though, that the nurses guessed what I had done, but did not mention a single word. Of course, they also had a good guess about the reason for my action: survival, even if taking a risk. I did gain some weight.

In my double room was another lady, beautiful Hillo, not much older than I. I shall always remember her with the greatest admiration and affection. She suffered from advanced TB, but no political prisoner received any medication.

She was superbly educated, enjoyed literature and poetry, and remembered several poems, many of which I memorized. Hillo was fond of the Chinese philosopher, Lao Tse from 600 B.C., and she shared her knowledge with me.

Like most of us, she was arrested for political reasons, without any proof. It was sad when I was separated from Inge and Gerdi over

Christmas 1949, but I felt spoiled rotten, having the great joy of piles of most loving Christmas mail from so very many kind people. Hillo and I told each other Christmas stories, talked about former Christmases with our loved ones, recited Christmas poems, and sang Christmas songs.

Shortly after the New Year of 1950 had sent the old one into retirement, I finally allowed the sores on my arms, legs, and torso to heal. Inge, Gerdi, and Hillo urged me not to ignore the great danger of blood poisoning any longer. I agreed and told myself that I really should not continue this dangerous game for too long, just for food. The goodbye from Hillo was very painful. I knew I would never see her again, considering her health condition, and I never did, but the reunion with all of my friends in the battalion was joyous. Besides, rumors circulated that most of us, except the Russian ladies, might get handed over to a German penal institution. Some Soviet, whose apartment our criminals cleaned, had dropped a hint. The promised November letter was canceled.

Even though no reason was given, it was a hint that something new was brewing. The battalion buzzed like a beehive! I heard new rumors every day. Many of those started with a guess; the next person might say, "I heard that" and for the next one, it became almost a fact. Some women with lower sentences started to promise friends what of their belongings the women would inherit.

They relished their plans about what would be the first things they intended to do in freedom. Eat good food was always number one on the list.

Another hint was Santa Claus. A cardboard figure of him, larger than life-size, arrived before Christmas and was propped up in the center of our battalion. A large certificate of release was protruding from his top-coat pocket. "Mockery, mockery" some of us, including me, commented. But still, everyone loved to see him and the dream world certificate.

Dad once said to me, "Unexpected allotments of fate make life more varied, maybe more interesting." Perhaps, there was some change coming. Whether positive or negative, that remained to be seen. The uncertainty did not last long. Once in a while, we received East German newspapers. Very few of us ever bothered reading this Communist trash, boasting of the marvelous progress being made in East Germany, such as removing the bomb damages and rebuilding all towns and cities. Almost none of this was the truth. But in West Germany, of course, what else? Everything was nothing but bad, the paper reported. The people had wrong traditions, habits, and customs, and the "unworthy" government passed wrong laws and incited against "honorable and peace-seeking" East Germany. But finally, there was something very interesting for all of us in the paper. Some of our pie-eyed women crashed down out of their dream world, and I thought again of Dad's words, "The higher you climb, the deeper you might fall." How true! The front page of one newspaper announced in large letters:

> The East German Government had been integrating into the Communists ideology, the true system of government so well that it could be trusted to take over some anti-communist prisoners. Others would be amnestied.

Those some turned out to be the majority: 5504 persons would be amnestied. These, no doubt, would be prisoners with lower sentences; for example, women who dated a Soviet soldier who deserted to the West, or women sentenced for anti-Soviet remarks, or prostitutes who had slept with a Soviet, or victims of someone who wanted to get rid of him or her, like Mrs. Finke. If you reported to the police that you heard someone make anti-communist statements, that was enough to arrest and sentence the poor victim. No further proof was necessary.

Three thousand, four hundred and thirty-two would be handed over to a German court of law for new sentencing. These were murderers and high-ranking former Nazis. The majority of 10,513 would be handed over to the East German Ministry of the Interior to continue their "justified and well-deserved" sentences in German jails. Six-hundred forty-nine citizens remained in Soviet hands, i.e., would end up in Siberia. These ladies were all Soviet citizens.

There were approximately eighteen thousand political and criminal inmates, including about thirteen hundred women in Sachsenhausen alone, which was by no means the only place of Soviet incarceration. Besides Bautzen and Brandenburg, there existed many others. Consequently, the numbers were very wrong. But the percentages alone made it pretty clear that we, Inge, Gerdi and I had not the slightest chance of going home. Our next trip would most likely be to a German camp or jail. Sachsenhausen was planned to be permanently closed.

West Germany had paid the Soviets an enormously high amount of money to release political prisoners with long sentences. The Soviets were delighted to take the money, but did you notice who went home? They promptly broke the agreement. But what else can you expect of communists? The next day, after we read the seemingly "scintillating" news, we were called to *Appell* during the day, and some Soviet officers told us the thing that was printed in the paper. I guess they were surprised again that there was no outcry of joy.

Even though we realized that freedom for us was out of reach now, a small spark of hope made us think: What did we do wrong against East Germany? Nothing. This Soviet-dominated dictatorship did not even exist in 1947! What reason could they possibly have to keep us incarcerated for the rest of our sentences? None. The underground organization to which Inge and I did not belong anyway, worked against the Soviets, not against East Germany. But our train of thought was very misguided because we had no idea that the Soviets kept the Germans completely in the dark. They were merely instructed to feed and watch us. They received no information about our "case," no details at all. The only facts the Soviets let them know were the alleged accusation in one word—espionage—and our sentences of twenty-five years. Consequently, the Communist German Police—convinced that their big brother never did anything wrong—regarded us as most dangerous criminals, who deserved no more than the strictest treatment, and that's exactly what lay ahead of us. Soon the day came when those lucky and overjoyed women who were amnestied gave away almost everything they owned. They were privileged to leave prison, breathe the air of freedom, and to return to their families. The murderers had already left us, facing German courts of law, and the Russian ladies were on their way to Siberia.

Finally, on February 11, 1950, the remaining rest of us were told to pack. That did not require much time. But what was I to do with my most precious pictures and mail? We all knew for certain that we would never be allowed to keep any of those. It was the saddest moment since my arrest, and I was sobbing when I burned all of my mail in our barrack's potbelly stove. Most of my photos suffered the same tragic fate, but not all of them. I hid a few in my underwear, hoping for a miracle. That miracle was on vacation that day. They found them when we had to strip naked. With a sadistic smile at me, she pitched them onto a pile of trash, next to the firewood. I could have strangled her on the spot!

Our third transport, on February 11, 1950, was in cattle cars again, like it was from Bautzen. But this time, our car was not overcrowded. No one had to lie on the floor. There were four large boards again. But it was beastly, unbearably cold, without any heat, some poor, poor women in light summer clothes had been arrested on a hot summer day. They had no sweater, no coat, and no one had any extra pieces of clothing to share with them. The only thing we could do for them was to huddle as close together as possible, which we did. This time, each of us received a package of food, including something we had not seen in two and one-half years: cold cuts and cheese. Was this a friendly goodbye from the Soviets?

It was a blessing that no one had to lie on the floor, of course. But another reason amused us: the toilet situation. Instead of a barrel, this time there was a relatively small hole in the floor in the center of the car. This was our toilet. It did not take the February frost long to close the hole completely. The result was similar to the cattle car from Bautzen. But now, in February, there was an ice skating opportunity, if there had not been so many obstacles in the ice. We tip-toed around them. This precipitated much entertainment and laughter among us!

After two days, we arrived in the small town of Stollberg in the Erzgebirge Mountains in southern Germany, about one hundred seventy-five kilometers (about one hundred eight miles) south of Berlin. Hoheneck was to be my new prison for almost six years, from February 11, 1950, to December 28, 1955.

HOHENECK

TRUCKS PICKED us up on February 12, 1950, at the railroad station of the small town of Stollberg in the Erzgebirge Mountains. Stollberg snuggles up on one side of a low mountain, on top of which sprawled a large building, 'Hoheneck.' It used to be a medieval fortress with an ideal location on the mountain; then it became a castle, then a monastery. In the nineteenth century, it was reconstructed to be used as a high-security prison for five hundred to six hundred prisoners. A closed courtyard was created by building a four-story-high cell house. We numbered 1119 women and thirty children born after the arrest of their mothers. The oldest child was about four years old; the youngest, a few months old. The oldest woman among us was seventy-six, a Herrenhut Lady. The Herrenhuts were a group of German volunteers who worked in Africa, helping people sick with leprosy. She told us very interesting but heartbreaking happenings during her work.

> "From 1945 to 1949, Soviet Military Tribunals (SMT) sentenced over thirty thousand Germans (for political reasons) to hard labor prisons, to death, or transported them to the Soviet Union as slave laborers, usually in Siberia."[1]

---

1. FINN, Gerhard, *Die Frauen von Hoheneck*, Westkreuz Publishing Co., Berlin pages 25, 52, 73.

With great joy, I saw a tree in the center. Its branches were bare, now, in February, but I was thinking ahead. Spring would come, and the tree would sprout green leaves. Loving nature as much as my Dad, I had not seen any tree since 1947. At least we had something with which to look forward to! Every one of us loved this tree, which reminded us that there were indeed trees, forests, and flowers outside of our walls. Maybe, just maybe, we would once again see Mother Nature's splendor someday in the future. It seemed to hold a promise for all of us.

We were greeted by a five-foot-tall policewoman in a blue uniform, with the words, "There you are, you trash. Unfortunately, you are still alive. I, myself, prefer murderers ten times over before you. They only killed one, or two, but you Nazis killed thousands." We were dumbfounded! We did not understand what she meant. This was Margarete Müller, (later married Suttinger), from 50 Hufeland Street in Stollberg. She was a plain policewoman when we arrived in Hoheneck. Due to her extraordinary communist loyalty, she retired with the rank of Colonel after the collapse of communism. One day, I heard her say, "What you did was the same as mass murder. If there were any justice from some God, you all would be long dead." In almost daily workshops, they, the police guards, were thoroughly brainwashed to believe that all anti-communists were all former Nazis, held responsible for the Holocaust and all Nazi atrocities. They were told that we had those extremely high sentences of twenty-five years because we all used to belong to the cream of the Nazis. Since only the lowest, uneducated scum of society volunteered for watching us, they were intellectually too inferior to have any opinion of their own. They were merely followers and believers.

Several prisoners sued Suttinger for her many years of inhumane cruelty after the collapse of communism in East Germany, in 1989. Nothing happened to her, absolutely nothing. There were many, too many former communists still in the eastern courts of law. She insisted that she only followed orders; all she had done was what she was instructed to do by her superiors. No punishment at all for her. All those lawsuits were thrown out.

We all were without the faintest idea about the reason for their hostile attitudes. After this "welcoming" and "kind" reception, we got a pretty good idea of what our future in Hoheneck would look like. Hoheneck had female guards only. I had not met a single male Soviet guard or officer behaving in such a vicious and beastly manner as those evil Communist bitches. It was their greatest joy to trample on our dignity, humiliating us whenever they saw any possibility to do so. The beatings of Mr. Tobartschikow were much easier for me to tolerate. In 1947 in Potsdam, I was aware of the fact that Germans had been his bitter enemies, destroying much of his country and annihilating many thousands of his countrymen. And the underground organization against the Soviets did exist.

But they let us keep the dignity of our names. That was too much of an honor for the German Communists. They immediately degraded us to nameless numbers. I was now Prisoner number 1247.

That's how they always addressed us, and it was the way we were taught to introduce ourselves to any guard; always, "Prisoner Number 1247 is humbly requesting to talk to you, madam." She then answered "No" or "Yes, you may, prisoner Number 1247." You can imagine how eager we were to ask for that permission. Someone asked when we could write to our families. Suttinger's answer was—I heard it—"You don't deserve such a privilege." All that hostile attitude was the result of constant brainwashing.

It was a great blessing that none of us had the faintest idea of how many inhumane, degrading comments, and how much disgusting, vile abuse we would have to endure for many endless years. For me, it was over in almost six years. In the beginning, we were full of hope that a German court might give us a new trial, which would reduce our high sentences so that they would be able to let us go home. It did not take very long until we realized that all communist police hated us without limit. Of course we did not know that the Soviets still held all reins firmly in their own hands. The Germans received absolutely no information about our 'cases'; they were merely supposed to keep us incarcerated and feed us. All they were allowed to know about us were the reason for our sentence (i.e. espionage) and the length (i.e. twenty-five years). That's all. That meant to the police "most serious offenders," and we had to be treated accordingly. They did.

Inge, Gerdi & I were sent to the north wing into day-room G-l, together with one hundred forty-seven others. Many long wooden tables with benches on both sides greeted us there. The washroom offered many basins, but with cold water only. There was a small waiting line at the basins in the morning. But at the toilet, it was a rare gift if we ever could sit in peace. This so-called "toilet" consisted of a wooden board with two large holes, on which we sat. Two wide, sloping pipes led from the holes down into large barrels. For a little extra food, prisoners lifted the barrels onto a cart which they pushed and pulled by hand to somewhere where the contents were dumped. There was no curtain, and the waiting comrades almost touched our knees in this very small room. They urged you, "Come on, let's go. You must be finished by now, don't fall asleep . . ." laughing, we took this all in stride. But we got angry whenever there was a strong wind, and our excrement ended up flying back up the pipe instead of landing in the barrel, which stood in the open air. But there was no running water to clean up there: we had to go to the washroom to do that.

Every evening, during this February 1950, we had to undress in our dayroom. All belongings except for underwear had to be placed on our bench in a perfectly neat pile. If it was not neat enough, the whole pile was swept down to the floor by the guard and remained there. Not even socks were allowed. "You could escape in socks," we were told. This was so utterly ridiculous we did not even smile because after we had crossed the courtyard, we climbed up to the 5th floor of the south wing. This was the attic above the cells, where flimsy straw sacks filled with chaff, waited for us in double bunk beds, each with one thin blanket. Our blankets from home had to remain in G-l. When we arrived in Hoheneck, in the winter of 1949/50, this attic without any heating was brutally cold. Many of us were coughing and sneezing, but Inge and I were spared. In the summer, however, the heat (this was directly under the roof) was so bad that many of us slept naked. Even though we were very thirsty, we waited until the next morning to get a drink, because neither Inge nor I would touch the rancid drinking water in a rusty barrel. We also avoided the second dirty barrel, the "toilet," as most of us did. Up high, close to the ceiling, we could not look out. The attic had tiny, tiny windows, maybe eight inches square, with thick iron bars cemented into the walls. These windows were not over the beds but in the opposite wall, south side wall. The beds were all along the north side wall. Escape from that attic? Utterly absurd, ludicrous, impossible!

It was very difficult but most important to keep as clean as possible. Illness without any treatment meant sure death. Therefore, we all washed our whole bodies naked, every day, summer and winter, even with ice-cold water. Many sinks were lined up, side by side, in the washroom. One day, a guard said to another one, "Look, those pigs wash themselves naked." There was not always water available for us. In the winter the pipes froze. In the summer the water pressure from Stollberg was too weak to reach up to our fortress on the mountain.

Water trucks came up, but the small amount of drinking water distributed to us left us thirsty. It is amazing what the human body is capable of enduring.

Breakfast consisted of a small piece of dry bread with black coffee. Almost all of the few criminals among us were now called to go to work, either in the kitchen or laundry room or outside the big wall in the guards' quarters and the large assembly rooms.

The guards, especially the beastly Müller, looked forward to our daily evening march through the inside courtyard in winter to get from our Day Room B1 (north side) to our attic (south side). This was such a good opportunity to bully us brutishly. Even if there had been dead silence, they made us stop walking. "I heard someone speak," she said and went back into the warm guards' room. She left us standing there, freezing to icicles in our underwear, for twenty to thirty minutes. I often wondered how older women among us could survive treatments like that. It was intolerable and unbearable for us young ones. Naturally, even our young bodies could not warm up without several blankets, all night long. The guards in the warm room looked at us through the window, laughing, obviously deriving sadistic pleasure out of our misery. I could have strangled them with my bare hands! Also, the question crossed my mind, how much of my twenty-five-year sentence would I be able to survive in Hoheneck?

Hoheneck's soup for dinner was almost the same quality as Potsdam's. It usually sported a few more leaves of cabbage, potatoes and often maggots. We fished them out, at first, and decorated the edge of our bowls with them. But soon, some lady said, "I don't care what you all think of me. I eat them just like the natives do because I am so terribly hungry and they give me a tiny bit of protein." We looked at each other, nodded, and ate our maggots. There was never any trace of meat in our soup. The kitchen crew, who were all criminals, ate most of that. Since the dayroom had no shutters, we observed guards taking home large shopping bags, out of which sometimes sausages dangled.

A loud bell woke everyone up around 6:00, or so. No one of us still had a watch, and there were no clocks anywhere. After our march back to Dayroom G-l, the daily stampede to the toilet and washroom followed. Not all the guards were of Müller's type. There was a young one who became a friend with a prisoner, which was almost a crime in the Communist's eyes. But when she offered to mail a letter to the prisoner's parents, this was a punishable crime. Another guard, an informer, had noticed something suspicious and reported it. The young guard was searched, and the letter was found. This was deemed an "act of treason." She was sentenced to ten years of incarceration in Hoheneck. But the prisoner, also very young, was afraid that her parents might get punished, and tried to avoid that by hanging herself, like Gerda Schumacher. At that time, we no longer had our private clothing. She tore her bedsheets in strips to make the noose. Another kind guard was caught when she tried to smuggle some food into a cell. She also ended up as a prisoner in Hoheneck.

It had become spring, and we watched joyfully and impatiently for our beloved tree, a linden tree in the courtyard to produce the first delicate sprouts, which would then turn into leaves. But in 1955, some of us had teary eyes when we noticed that this perfectly healthy tree was sentenced to die. When the killing rope tore, and the tree still stood upright, a loud cry of joy erupted from the day-rooms, which had no shutters on their windows. But nothing helped; we lost our tree. They used a chain instead of a rope.

After they had disrobed us of our names and replaced them with numbers, it did not take long until they took away all of our private clothing, which was sent home. Another step in molding us from individual people into faceless, nameless creatures. This was a blessing, however, for those of us who had been arrested in lightweight summer clothes, maybe years ago. Some of their outfits were torn and soiled. What could these poor women do about it? Neither the Soviets nor those German Police bitches cared. I hated to give up my warm pullover and thick, blue topcoat, with those treasures hidden in the shoulder padding.

When my clothes arrived at home, sent from Hoheneck, I wanted my parents to retrieve the snake ring and the blood letter, but this was difficult. It took me quite a lot of diplomatic skill and veiled hints to let my parents know why they should open the shoulder padding of my blue topcoat. I could not possibly write openly about my ring and 'blood letter' from Potsdam, hidden inside. No question about it, the Hoheneck administration would have stuck me into *Karzer* forever! I fooled them by using my middle name, Eleonore, and my parents understood: "If Eleonore's blue coat is getting too short for her since she grew a lot, why don't you take out the shoulder pads, which would lengthen the coat a bit." My parents found the ring and the letter, written in Potsdam with the blood of my fingertip. The ring used to be a present from my Godfather for my mother's confirmation. It was a snake, originally with a ruby in its forehead which had fallen out many years ago. Dad now had the missing ruby replaced with a diamond as a welcome-home gift for me. I have worn this ring every day since.

The Hoheneck *Karzer* in the basement of the cell house was a mild variety of a torture chamber without the physical torture. The *Karzer* in Potsdam was different. In Bautzen and Sachsenhausen there was no *Karzer*, as far as I know. This German invention was a windowless cell underground, in the basement of the house. These *Karzer* cells had two iron doors. The poor, usually innocent victim, received a warm meal every third day, but each morning and evening some black coffee. The flimsy straw sack on the iron bed frame had to be placed outside the cell door in the morning and remain there. The prisoner was "graciously" permitted to lie on the straw sack every second night. How thoughtful! There was never any *Rundgang* (fresh air walk in the inner, enclosed courtyard) for those poor victims. By always quietly trying to mingle in a crowd, if possible, Inge, Gerdi and I never experienced the "pleasure" of the Hoheneck *Karzer*.

Our new "elegant" Hoheneck wardrobe consisted of two men's Russian, striped flannel shirts without any collar because prisoners had hanged themselves. Using cigarettes to barter for collars, prisoners hanged themselves by attaching several collars. Two pair of men's long underwear substituted for any panties: no bra, but a headscarf which had to be worn anytime outside the cell or day-room. The underwear was exchanged every three weeks. After three and one-half years of uninterrupted daily wear, with rare opportunities to wash them hastily, our underwear was in pitiful condition. Our parents knew the reason for that from hidden hints in our mail from Sachsenhausen.

Our very coarse, rough, gray upper wear, pants, and a jacket were adorned with a brightly colored strip on arms, legs, and backs. Red for those who were regarded as dangerous, like murderers and women who attacked someone; yellow for petty criminals like thieves. All the rest were politicals, and we got green stripes. The daily sight of this dark gray monotony of our uniforms was depressing for us, at first. But after a while, we hardly noticed these abnormalities anymore. Being blessed with my Dad's positive outlook towards life, I said to Inge, "Well, so we do not have to wear out our own clothing anymore."

Even our shoes were taken away from us. They were replaced by short-shafted black boots without any shoe strings. We were told that we might strangle a guard with shoe strings even though they usually approached us in pairs. Ridiculous rules and regulations often went overboard. The artificial leather of the boots was so hard and thick that most of us ended up with sores on our feet. To pull up the foot rags was forbidden, but we did it whenever we were out of sight of any guard. The sole consisted of wood, one and one-half inches thick, which made normal walking impossible. We stomped as if through heavy snow.

It was miraculous how we could get used to such awkward, unnatural things and barely notice it anymore since all of us walked this way. After a short time, all of our arches under the feet were flat as a mirror. But many years later, the police 'graciously' paid us pennies for eight hours of daily work. Then they opened a small in-prison shop with candy, cigarettes, crèmes (facial), and shoes. It took a long time of saving, but finally Inge and I each got a pair of normal shoes. Inge's were brown, mine a sage green. I loved these shoes as one loves a rare toy. Quite unbelievable, what Mother Nature is capable of achieving! After having walked in our new shoes and without those horrible boots for a while, our arches did curve up into a normal position. We were also allowed to ask our parents for socks. Small but greatly appreciated steps towards normality, after many years.

A special highlight in our monotonous daily existence was the *Rundgang,* the allotment of fresh air in the courtyard. They must have had some order to give us some fresh air once in a while, for fifteen or twenty minutes. But often the guards were too lazy to let us out. When we left our cell or day room, a guard inspected our appearance. Everything had to be impeccable: kerchief on the head, all buttons on the jacket properly buttoned, no corner of a foot rag peeped out of the boot. The smallest violation meant: back to your cell or day room.

We had to walk in single file, with about two yards distance between us (so there was no speaking among us), heads down (so there was no eye contact with the windows), and hands had to be on your back (so no guard could be attacked). Never did any Soviet guard or officer treat us like this. Each day began with harassments, which they enjoyed, and ended with harassments. Peace was only when we were among ourselves unless two of us did not like each other. After a while, my emotions became stony. I built an invisible wall around myself, and all insults and provocations bounced off that as if the wall was made of granite. The Soviets had arrested us because they knew that we were their bloody enemies. The Germans, however, had no such reason. The Soviets never tried to crush our human dignity. We arrived in Hoheneck as dignified women. But the Germans did everything possible to mold us into groveling, cowering, intimidated slaves. Mrs. Suttinger said one day, "We shall crush your pride; just wait, we shall mold you into cringing drudges. And this will not take us long." They never succeeded! We acted like obedient slaves, but our posture was upright, proud, heads held high. How they hated that! By following their commands promptly, we robbed them of the satisfaction they derived out of punishments. We would have walked barefoot back to the Soviets in Bautzen or Sachsenhausen at any time.

One day during *Rundgang*, I detected a small piece of broken glass on the ground. This was almost as valuable as a knife. At the next round, I stepped a little aside of our single-file parade, bent over as if I had to stuff a corner of my foot rag back into my boot and picked up the glass. I waited to get back into my former place in the circle, but the guard yelled at me, "Get back in line, you piece of trash." That bounced off my granite wall. What was important was I had the glass. The most reliable and effective method of survival was to hide, if possible, in a group of prisoners, never to attract any guard's attention, always obey promptly and without any question, never contradict, never speak unless asked, and never show any feeling or emotion. This way, we gave them no opportunity to say or do anything nasty, with no other reason but to hurt our feelings. They loved to separate relatives and friends, like the three Schulze sisters. Therefore, Inge and I continued to avoid showing them any sign of friendship but pretended to be strangers.

The first commander of Hoheneck was by far the worst one, coming up with stricter and stricter rules and regulations. One day he crossed the courtyard while I had *Rundgang*. A very unwise prisoner stepped out of her line to talk to him. His screaming answer was "Sprechen Sie mich nicht an." "Don't you dare talk to me." This sentence was in such an incredible low-gutter German and grammatically so wrong that it was hard for the rest of us not to grin, at least. We just bent our heads down even farther. Later, we used his inconceivably bad German as a joke among us. This repulsive, vulgar man must have had his cradle sitting in the lowest possible gutter of society.

In April of 1950, he came up with the idea that all prisoners with a twenty-five-year sentence, being the worst of all politicals, did not deserve the privilege and freedom of a day room, but should all be in cells. The idea was conceived and carried out right away. I was among the first to be transported from our G-l into cell number twenty-five with a concrete floor, (the first floor). There were tiny peepholes in the wooden boards in front of the window, through which one could peek into the courtyard. I occupied such a hole and waited for Inge to leave our G-l. Then I pressed my ear against my door and detected some commotion in the hallway. The guards did not know what to do; all the cells were already overloaded. They had jammed five prisoners into cells with only two beds, equal to one bunk bed. Each cell had a metal flag which popped out into the hallway if a prisoner pushed a button inside when he/she wanted or needed attention. That is like the flag which the "Devil" pushed to tell a guard about the hidden treasures (ring and letter) in the shoulder padding of my topcoat. I pushed the button and pounded against my door. When a guard opened the door, I told her that Inge was my cousin and that I was willing to share my straw sack with her. They were happy to get rid of at least one of the burdensome surplus. Inge came into my cell, and we were together again. I had beaten them! In cell twenty-five, the window could not be opened. Therefore, the walls were covered with moisture, at spots even mold, which gave the cell a smelly, musty odor. There was, of course, no sink but the usual stinking potty. A very thick heating pipe ran from the uppermost floor down to the first floor. It was not always warm, seldom hot, but it served us wonderfully for communicating upwards and downwards with the other floors, using our alphabet-knocking system as I explained earlier.

Our wall-knocking system enabled us to learn the sad, finally tragic story of our comrade Gerda Schumacher, our neighbor in cell twenty-six. In the spring of 1950, some of us in day room G-1 were "graciously" given the privilege of a little work, which was normally a priority of criminal prisoners. Loaves of bread had to be carried from the bakery trucks, which stood in the inner courtyard, to the food supplies room. One bread loaf disappeared. No one would have noticed that. But the prisoners divided the chunks of bread between each other, unaware of the tragic event that followed the discovery of breadcrumbs on the stairs to the food supply room. They had no unobserved time to clean up. A guard noticed the crumbs. The entire G-l received no food at all for one day. They hand-picked other prisoners for unloading the bread permanently. Gerda Schumacher was among those. One of the drivers of the truck took pity on the skinny, hungry women, who had mentioned the cruel, inhumane treatments of the guards. The driver whispered to Gerda that he had hidden a package of sandwiches for her to take! All prisoners could at any time, reason or not, be singled out by any guard for a body search. Gerda had the terrible bad luck to be one of those, and the package was found, of course, solitary confinement in cell twenty-six and countless hearings. The cruel Head Commander of Hoheneck was most anxious to find out which one of the drivers had committed this "rebellious, mutinous, criminal act" (against Communist East Germany). It revealed so much hostility against the government, they said, that he must be sentenced to prison. Gerda knew that he had a family and children at home. She took it upon herself to insist that she had stolen the package out of the truck. A big assembly of all prisoners in the courtyard followed. Gerda stood in the center on a small, raised platform. The Commandant made a speech accusing her of that terrible crime she had committed. She was sure that some of the prisoners believed that she was a thief, and she ran the gauntlet walking by the guards who said the nastiest things to her.

Two days later, at night, she hanged herself from the heating pipe with her leather belt. We still had our private clothes, then. After this, no belts with the uniforms. Her parents received a letter stating that their daughter, (to their greatest pity) had suffered a fatal heart attack. She had been cremated, but the urn was not available. Gerda was not cremated. After the collapse of communism, her bones were found and identified buried outside of the prison wall. The parents then received the bones for a proper burial. After a short time, the truth was passed on to all prisoners by wall-knocking. But the news of her suicide had to be reported to the masters, the Soviets. The cruel first commandant was replaced, and our daily lives changed with some unexpected improvements and more food.

We did not seriously feel sorry for Gerda—she no longer had to suffer through the humiliating mistreatment of the guards. Many of us would have had the courage to follow her example. But the strong sense of duty to our families, waiting so desperately to see us back home among them, and the strong will to spare them the terrible grief over the loss prevented all of us from following Gerda's example.

Soon, we saw our new commander, Chief Officer Reitz, to whom the guards behaved very respectfully. He introduced several significant, positive changes in Hoheneck. In July 1952, Officer Reitz thought teenagers and young people should not vegetate in small, overcrowded cells. He gave orders to move us back into a dayroom. Unfortunately, the cut-off date was 1927-1928. I moved into teenagers' dayroom G-3, but Inge, 1927, ended up in G-4. It took three months and countless applications and pleas until I finally was allowed to move to G-4. I had been very unhappy and annoyed among all those saucy, impertinent youngsters without proper behavior or respect. (Many of them were common thieves.) Inge and I were happy to be back together in the north wing dayroom.

Now, at the beginning of summer, it was no longer so lousy cold to sleep in the attic. The food became a little better, and there seemed to be a little more of it. The *Rundgang* was more relaxed and regular, with less screaming. It included gymnastic exercises taught by an inmate gym teacher. Officer Reitz even allowed us to play volleyball outside of the workshops in the west wing. We were most grateful for all the fresh air and the sunshine. Maybe, that was what saved Inge's life. In cell twenty-five, x-rays had shown a shadow on her lung. We were extremely worried that it might develop into tuberculosis. The quality and scarcity of food and the lack of fresh air after Sachsenhausen prohibited improvement. Thank God, she never did develop tuberculosis, which would have been her death.

After countless requests from our families, directed to the head-quarters in East Berlin and the Soviets, we were permitted to write a postcard home. On May 6, 1950 (preceded by many rules about what not to mention) we sent cards home. We were so very happy to be able to relieve our parents after eight and a half months, from their great worry of not knowing our whereabouts. A little later, we wrote a second post-card, bringing our families the great joy of knowing that we were now allowed to receive one food package, once a month, of not more than six pounds. There were some restrictions about what was forbidden to send, like knives, forks, nail files, needles, etc. But most of us received mainly food and some personal items. When we were allowed to receive our first package from home, our families were not fully instructed about what we were permitted to get and what not. Coffee, tea, cocoa, and alcohol were forbidden. It is really difficult to believe the police's unique idea. They had a choice to return these items to the sender. That would have required them to re-pack them, and it would have cost mailing post-age. Much more convenient was a second choice from some old police guide book. A few of us were taken to the kitchen. There was the pile of the forbidden items. The prisoners dumped all of them except alcohol in a big kettle with some water in it. This coffee/tea/cocoa—soup was boiled a little while, cooled, and then the alcohol was added. Now it was ready to be offered to the general prison population, as the guide book required. It was too difficult to do that in the cell houses, but not in the day rooms. I cannot tell how this strange soup tasted, because I was in the cell house at that time. But the dayroom people who tried it said that is was certainly most unusual but not bad.

Inge and I could not believe our eyes, seeing all those delicacies from our packages in front of us. There were cold cuts, bacon, chocolate, honey from Dad's beehives, a small cake, cookies, raisins, and apples, as well as wonderful-smelling soap and skin cream and toothpaste. We did not touch anything of our treasures, just looked at them for a few days. The mere thought that our loved ones had touched and had lovingly wrapped each item made our hearts beat faster. Our parents asked us in their next letter what we would like to get, if not forbidden. Inge and

I had a new idea! There was no color in our lives; everything was gray. We yearned for face cloths—the luxury of which we had to do without for three years—face cloths in the brightest colors. We got them! Mine sported a very cute, large Mickey Mouse appliqued on it. We were the envy of everyone! We had hidden our precious new face cloths under our towels, but that was not good enough. It took just one or two days. The guards saw us using them, and they took them. To whom could a prisoner complain, who would listen? Officer Reitz would not ever have seen an application to talk to him about this thievery. He would not have received any letter from us either.

From June 1950 on, we were permitted to write and to receive a fifteen-line letter, once a month, unless we were sentenced to no mail because of having violated some house rule. A foot rag may have peeped out of the edge of a boot, or the jacket was not buttoned with all its buttons, or the kerchief had slipped on to the back of the neck, or the prisoner had spoken without having been asked. Both our own and our family's mail again were decorated with blackened-out sentences or paragraphs, like it was at Sachsenhausen. In cases of no mail, letters were returned to the senders without any explanation, but this never happened to us. It was very difficult to find the right words to make our parents believe that we were well taken care of and more or less without worries. After all, our world consisted of nothing but mistreatment and hunger. But they worried about us so much all the time, anyway, and could do nothing at all to help us. In front of our eyes, all packages were thoroughly examined in the administration building, and I mean thoroughly! Cakes, cold cuts, ham, oranges, lemons, etc. were chopped up before the pieces were dumped back into the packages. For many of us, like Inge, this was the first time in years that they did not have to borrow a comb or toothbrush from some compassionate soul. We all enjoyed so much those long missed treats of lovely-smelling body creams, soap, and toothpaste. The guards gave us some soap, but it was half loam, without any fragrance and produced no suds. Even my Latin teacher, a longtime friend of our family, Dr. Hutloff, usually sent me a cervelat sausage or he sent me hard salamis. My uncle in Hamburg sweetened our-sweet tooth with chocolate in every package. I was always amazed at how many relatives and friends contributed items to show their love.

At home, it was also a great joy for our parents to pack the packages for us, even though it also was a great nuisance to weigh each item and calculate the weight of the wrapping, so they adhered to the six-pound limit. Inge and I had joint-kitchen privileges; all of mine was hers and vice versa. Whenever one of our parent's birthdays was approaching, we saved the best from the packages for a celebration in our cell or the dayroom with friends. My Dad lovingly brought the first package to Hoheneck himself, which happened on his wedding anniversary. In his usual optimism, he hoped that he could persuade the guards to allow him to hand the package to me himself. But of course, he did not know the strict, unbreakable Communist rules which had to be carried out by obedient, and brainwashed slaves.

Dad circled the castle many times, anxious to see my face, but I was in a cell at that time. I had no idea that he was so close to me! There was no mercy regarding the requested weight of the packages. Too heavy meant that the packaged was returned. This happened to me, but I did not know it then. My parents took something out, sent it again, and I was allowed to have it.

A horrible catastrophe lay ahead of all our inmate mothers with a child who had been born in prison. One by one, they were taken to our ambulance (health services), which, they were told, was for a routine medical examination. All of our doctors and nurses were political prisoners. A guard separated all the children from their mothers, who were taken back to their day rooms. The explanation given was logical: No child should grow up in prison. But there was no answer to the question of where their children were taken. They were taken to nurseries or children's homes, some of them in the Soviet Union, and they were given new names unless the child had a father or grandparents living outside. I wonder whether some of the mothers ever found their child again.

I also can imagine the often tragic difficulties of starting to bond after the mothers returned home after six, seven, or eight years. A child faced a totally strange woman if raised in an orphanage or children's home, and was expected to call her "mother." The child may never have seen a picture of his mother; no one may have mentioned her, or even the word "mother." We know that in several cases, a loving mother-child relationship could never be established. Lucky were those children who had a father, grand-parents, or relatives who took them in and raised them. It was especially difficult for the child if he/she had been raised in one of Stalin's Soviet nurseries and brainwashed for years with Communist ideas and idols.

I could never figure out why they forced us into the frequent Verlegungen (changes from the cell house to a dayroom and then back into a cell). Maybe they wanted to avoid building too-close friendships and group building! But a total, three-day hunger strike, including all prisoners, happened anyway, years later. Most of the time, Inge and I somehow managed to stay together. Sometimes luck helped, sometimes our close age, and later, the same workplace and shift.

It finally dawned on the administration that all those slaves, political prisoners, ought to be used to put money into Hoheneck's coffers by making them produce something, unpaid of course! They began making preparations for that to happen.

Among all of those brainwashed guards in Hoheneck, there was a sunbeam. We just had not yet met her. Inge and I stayed in a cell on the first floor at that time, together with Waltraud Schmidt, a woman of our age and our case, innocent but sentenced to the customary twenty-five years. We got along well together. One day in the spring of 1950, the cell door was opened at an unusual time. A new guard entered and asked us whether one of us knew how to embroider. My hand flew up! I immediately was thinking of the treasures which would be in our cell, like needle and thread for small repairs—like the button on Heinz's pants—and a pair of scissors! What a treasure to cut hair and nails. My mother and grandmother had done embroidery, and I had watched them with great interest. Mom once had even wanted to become a home economics teacher. I had to do very small projects for my home economics classes in school. The next day, the guard, whom we called 'our blond angel' came with a new white bed sheet and the necessary utensils. She wanted it changed to a tablecloth with a pretty edge. I was delighted because

I could foresee no problem with that. She informed us that no guard would confiscate any of the supplies because she had applied for permission to have it done. We were the happiest three prisoners in Hoheneck, and I joyfully started on my job.

A few days later, our 'blond angel' asked us whether we could crochet a baby jacket. I would not have had the courage to volunteer for that, but Inge did. That was incredibly bold! They talked about the size and Inge drew with her finger something on the cell floor. "You need a piece of paper to do that," the guard said, "and I shall stay here while you draw the pattern. We shall then cut out the pattern, and I shall take the rest of the paper and the pencil with me so that you don't get in any trouble." This would have been enough to sentence her to jail for disloyalty to their Communist rules and regulations. Several years later, she was sentenced to jail for being too friendly with two other political prisoners. She was considered not faithful to the political party ideology and sentenced to jail at Hoheneck.

Inge had finished her baby jacket, but I was still working on my tablecloth. When I was finished with the edge, I suggested accenting the edge with a large center embroidery. She was excited! The roof of the cell house consisted of slates, which can be written on with a pebble. Pieces of slates lay in the courtyard. A little angel from above helped me to keep the courtyard guard's attention focused in another direction, so that I was able to pick up a piece of slate (and later a pebble), and hide them under my jacket. It took me a long time to draw a center motif, erase it, draw it again. When our angel came on duty, she loved my design. Not only at the time of our work projects, but also afterward, our blond angel secretly and carefully sneaked little goodies like fruit into our cell, and she allowed us forbidden privileges such as sleeping during daytime, whenever she was on duty. Finally, my center motif was completed, but I hated to give up the tablecloth and all our little 'treasures.' I suggested to her we create four identical motifs on a much smaller scale for the four corners. She loved the idea. I could not possibly think of anything else to cling to that tablecloth. It had indeed become a valuable piece of art. Our 'blond angel' brought many of her colleagues to our cell to show them my creation when it was almost finished. I cried after I finally had to hand it over to her. Most painful for me was my unsolvable desperation. How I yearned to be able to give it to my mom. I knew, of course, that I never, ever in my life, would be able to see it again; it did not belong to me. If ever I was destined to survive this incarceration, I would never find such a tremendous amount of leisure time to recreate this tablecloth. I had been working on my project for several months, daily, from breakfast until bedtime. My eyes had been perfect then; I had to count the threads in the material for every single stitch!

One day, during August 1950, a guard came to our cell at an irregular time and took Inge, Waltraud, and me to the west wing. Different kinds of workshops had been created there. This was the welcome day on which our monotonous daily cell life ended. We did not care much that we were now unpaid slave laborers. Time goes by faster if you can work on a project. We had been assigned to be nail producers (called NILOS), and that was not the worst of the work. I was glad that we were not assigned to load the big barrels under the day-room toilets onto carts. Enormous thick cables had been brought to Hoheneck, possibly overseas cables. A large machine cut them into one or two-yard pieces. The cables consisted of many thick or thin steel wires twisted around each other many times. Our first task was to separate the wires until we ended up with just one twisted wire. We did that outside of the building and received the appropriate tools. They had selected young inmates because it was a pretty hard job, but it was in the sun! (There were always several guards watching us, but none of us would have attacked them, i.e., lifelong sentence). The next step took us into the workshop.

We had to hit the twisted wires with small hammers until they were straight as a pencil. After we had cut the wires in whatever length they needed the nails to be, those pieces traveled to the grinders, who were sitting at small grindstones, on which they ground pointed tips onto each nail-embryo. Finally, these headless *rigils* ended up on Inge's and my table for the finishing step. Sitting on the table we squeezed each nail, point down, into an anvil, and hit the top with our hammer for a long time, until the steel warmed and softened a bit, and we could form a little head. We kept this job for three years because no one else wanted to do it. Many tried, guards too, but no one ever achieved a head. We had learned little tricks so that we produced several hundred nails daily. We were happy at our job for several reasons. We got a little more food than non-workers; we were not pushed and pestered to achieve a given quota. We had no competition: no one succeeded in producing a nail with a head! And most of all, they needed Inge and me. Nails were hard to get in East Germany. The workshop for shoe repairs for the guards depended on us, and so did the woodworking shop. Our nails were also used in the construction of a new house for the guards' amusements—films, entertainments. There was never any reclamation or complaint about our work. So very many hammers hitting the steel caused an unimaginable noise beyond description. In the beginning, we stuffed something into our ears, but still needed a while to get used to it. But all the guards stayed in our shop just for minutes, another job advantage! And we had a kind, friendly, male guard.

Once a male policeman from our woodworkers' shop who had unsuccessfully tried to produce a nail head, asked us how we have possibly managed to not go insane with that tedious, boring job, day after day, month after month, year after year. This presented no problem at all for us, because we memorized something every day, usually poems which somebody remembered. We stuffed our heads with beauty—beautiful poems, meaningful words. No one could forbid it or take away from us. This enriched us, and they could do nothing about it. One English teacher among us had memorized in freedom all thirty-four pages of Rainer Maria Rilke's poem in rhythmic prose "Cornet."

It took quite a while, but Inge and I learned even all of that. Long after we were no longer *Nilos, comrades* asked us to recite it for them. Several places in the text fitted into our life, like normal, regular letters in "comrades"

Rast, Gast sein einmal.
Nicht immer feindlich nach allem fassen.
Einmal sich alles geschehen lassen und wissen:
Was geschieht, ist gut.

Auch der Mut muss einmal sich strecken . . ."

Translates to:
A rest, to be a guest for once!
Do not always reach for everything with hostility
Just for once, let things happen to me,
Knowing whatever happens will be good.
Even courage has to take a stretch, once in a while.

There were a few among us who pretended—or not pretended—to be mentally not quite normal. Usually, they got away unpunished with what they did, and the rest of us had wonderful entertainment! One of those ladies had been assigned to be *Küblerin*. They had to replace the full barrel under the day-room toilets with an empty one and put the full one on a little cart to dump it. Our comrade selected the right moment, pretended to trip, and let go of her grip on the full barrel, so that much of the contents sloshed all over the guard's legs and feet.

The prisoner showed the deepest regret and was not punished. Another one of such incidents happened in the pig's barn. A group of officers came to Hoheneck to check out this and that. They also went to the pig's barn. The guards fattened the pigs with leftovers, but we never got any of that, like in Bautzen. One of us was a countrywoman who had worked with pigs all her life. She placed herself at the other end of the barn, raised a big metal fork and ran to the officers screaming, "Don't you dare to do anything to my pigs!" They smiled, turned around, and left.

Another quite funny incident happened on New Year's Eve of 1953/54. All of the bunk beds in the attic above the cells stood at the north wall; the few small windows were located on the roof of the South wall. Somebody came up with the idea that if we push our legs through the bars and hang them to the outside, our legs would be in freedom, and maybe the rest of us will follow! Idea conceived and carried out. They pushed a bunk bed from the northside to the south, and just about everyone wanted to hang her legs out. There were so many of us on this upper bed that it crashed down onto the lower bed. No one got hurt or punished. Those beds were not built very solidly in the first place, and no guard could prove the next morning, that any of the beds had been moved.

It was in the fall of 1950 when an announcement was made that all prisoners, except for spies with a sentence of twenty-five years shall be allowed to receive a thirty-minute visit from one family member every three months. That was a hard blow for us. But luckily a second announcement followed: Officer Reitz exempted young spies under twenty-five years of age. We danced in unlimited joy, and so did our parents. Officer Reitz must have had children because he allowed us young ones to see even both of our parents. October 30th was this glorious, happy day.

Inge and I counted the hours in greatest excitement and feverish anticipation. Three years had passed since our arrest. Would our parents look marked by grief? They did in the photos which we got from them in Sachsenhausen. But not now. The great joy of seeing each other was beaming over all our faces; waves of happiness flooded over us from head to toe! There was a very large table between us, on which an eight to ten-inch high barrier was mounted in the center. A very unfriendly female guard who refused to answer my Dad's questions watched them and me with great attention. I had been a schoolgirl when I had to leave them in 1947. Now I was an adult with much ability to judge human nature and plenty of unusual life experiences. But, in spite of all, the loving contact between our hearts was unchanged. And how extremely hard did they try to spoil me! Even though I was not permitted to take any part of their gifts back to my cell, I so very much enjoyed admiring the beautiful flowers they had brought for me. Was it three years since I had seen a flower? Like my parents, I had always loved flowers, the woods; all of Mother Nature.

Mom had brought my favorite beverage, cocoa, in a thermos bottle and some sweets, which I was permitted to enjoy, but not to take some with me for Inge. Too much generosity! I was so deeply touched by my parents' great love and caring. If love and caring is a normal, daily occurrence, it often is not valued enough, maybe not even recognized. But for us, it was replaced with yelling, our dignity being trampled on by meanness and hatred. Therefore, we were abnormally sensitive to and grateful for loving warmth.

Every thirty minutes eventually comes to an end. At this first visit, we were still allowed to hug each other over the barrier on the table. Unfortunately, this little freedom had been abused by someone smuggling some small item or paper from one to the other — result: No more hugs, ever. The cruel moment of separation came, and the door closed behind the two most beloved persons in my life. I was ushered back to my cell, and our ugly, colorless, gray existence continued.

I was again thinking of Rilke's "Cornet." "To be a guest . . ." I was very grateful that God allowed me to be the 'guest' for thirty minutes. These few minutes with my beloved parents gave me the strength and patience to endure whatever form the mistreatments took. They waited just as impatiently as we did to be together again, someday. We had just been united for a few minutes, but now I had to bear with over five more years without them. However, now we had the heartwarming memory of our visit. Inge and I were blessed to have both parents alive and well.

Our ignorance about the future was a blessing. Officer Reitz's little favor to allow 'young spies' a visit was canceled from headquarters, and we had no more visits for twenty months. But after this temporary ban, I enjoyed ten more visits before I finally was amnestied. Some more food in Hoheneck did make me look not so skinny anymore, Mom and Dad were no longer worried. My body recognized the improvement by feeling strong enough to restart my monthly menstruation in January 1951, after four and a half years.

Of course, it was very difficult for us to find enough old rags; although they gave us some feminine napkins, it was just not enough. Old winter with his snow caps on our linden tree, (which was still living at this time) had to move into hibernation. Young spring came galloping to us in huge strides. It brought us the joy of watching the first leaves being born. Summer followed, and Inge and I still hammered heads on nails. July 24 was my parent's silver wedding anniversary, which they decided not to celebrate without me, postponing it until I was back home. Inge surprised me with the idea of asking her parents to buy a flower arrangement in my name and have it delivered with their flowers on that day. I would reimburse them later. Her parents were happy to do it, and my parents had a nice surprise. There was no celebration, but Gebi, friends, and neighbors brought so many flowers that a corner of our garden was like a picture of a sea of flowers. Much later, I saw the snapshot. I applied to Officer Reitz for special permission to write an anniversary letter home. He approved it. Inge and I celebrated this anniversary our way. We had saved from our latest packages the very best of the treats, and enjoyed them, then, with our cellmate, Waltraud.

Gebi had finished his studies at the University of Rostock this summer. He passed all his exams, received his bachelor's degree, and the university offered him a job as an instructor; later, as a professor, which he accepted.

He was thirty-four by now. It was hard for me to understand that a man like he, intelligent, healthy, good looking, with a spotless character and ethics, and now also holding an excellent position, would still refuse to date anyone else. But he insisted on waiting for me. In October 1951, we had been separated for four years. But my urging him to find someone else kept falling on deaf ears, even though no one knew whether I would even survive Hoheneck. He could and should have been happily married with children, having a family of his own. I felt guilty for ruining his life, but what else could I do besides asking him to find a wife? Whenever he visited Frankfurt/Oder he spent more time with my parents than with his own. Neither of my parents had suggested it, but he asked them for permission to call them 'Mom' and 'Dad.'

The Christmas letter of 1951 from my parents still had the usual five lines from Gebi, but they were not quite as loving and tender as before. In January, his five lines were missing. My parents first ignored my questions. But they could not keep it a secret forever. Gebi got engaged to the daughter of a college professor and stopped all contact with my parents. They were extremely upset when he visited them, breaking this news. They really should have guessed, because Gebi asked them in a letter in December not to get a Christmas present for him. They returned the new watch which they had bought for him.

I was not that much upset like they feared. I was sad, of course, but also a little relieved that I no longer carried the burden and fear that I might ruin his future and his life. I also told myself that neither of us were seniors in high school anymore, but adults with many different life experiences. Were we still suited to each other in a marriage? He remained just 'engaged' for more than four years; the wedding was, unknown to him or me, on December 30, 1955, just two days after my amnesty from Hoheneck. He made sure that his marriage remained childless, much to the objection of his wife. Many years later, I visited them from America twice. Gebi passed away in 2015.

The visitation ban for spies was lifted, and our fathers, with much effort, got permission for a double-date visit for Inge and me, so that we saw our fathers in the same room. This made the goodbye just a little bit less painful. Madam Hempel conducted herself quite caustically. These guards must have found a lot of satisfaction in harassing and pestering us. Our dads were unable to say anything about that, but afterward, my dad always called her 'the blond poison.'

Dad showed me the new, elegant, golden watch that they had bought as a homecoming present. He also showed me the camelhair material which they had purchased for a new winter coat for me. All of my top clothes from 1947 were much too short now (big change in fashion). The beast of a guard at the visit did not permit me to touch either the watch nor the material. Pure harassment!! Dad was very angry at that behavior, but remained civil, of course. Dad was always a model of an optimist, believing in an amnesty for us. Unfortunately, this was four years in the future. Thank God, both Mom and Dad were still alive, then.

As happy news from home, I learned that Dad had started a new business, a de-rusting enterprise. His previous downtown business was leveled by bombs and fire, like the entire center of Frankfurt/Oder, ninety-five percent. Almost all inhabitants had been evacuated, and the German military had started to withdraw. Large equipment and machines were exposed to the elements for many months and had rusted. Dad bought some property, had all the rubble removed, had big holes excavated like giant bathtubs, and then had them filled with some liquid chemical. After big cranes had immersed the rusted machines into the chemical, the rust was removable without too much effort.

One day, a little old lady showed up with a rusted little pressing iron in hand. She told Dad that rain onto the rubble of her house had ruined it. Could he de-rust it? Dad was amused, but of course, did not charge her anything for the little job. He also bought her a new iron. Dad's new business grew so fast and was so successful that he decided to start the reconstruction of our big twelve apartment house which had been so severely bomb-damaged that no apartment could be occupied, and neither the pharmacy nor the small dry-goods shop could be utilized. He was able to rent the first apartment in October of 1952. I knew how Communism had blossomed since the Soviets force-fed the East Germans with their philosophy. They found many willing, obedient followers who tried all imaginable tricks and ways of persuasion to steal property and businesses so that the government could pocket it. Years later, this happened to Dad, but in 1952, our eternal optimist still believed that it could not get worse. It did! In 1952 and 1953, he spent over fifty thousand marks (approximately $25,000) for material and labor to have his apartment house completely rebuilt. I could not understand that at all! The city government watched his enormous efforts and found it quite interesting given the future possibility of stealing it all! So, they found a way of doing just that. However, many decades later, after his death, his efforts paid off, and I was the one who profited. Sorry, Dad, I should have believed in you. When Communism collapsed in 1989, and the Berlin Wall fell, former real estate and business owners could request from the new democratic government or city administration the return of their former property. Since both of my parents were deceased, I was the sole heir, and all real estate was returned to me. Dad's business, however, had been sold to another private owner and could not be reclaimed.

The August 1952 letter from my parents consisted of several pieces. A total of four lines had been cut out at different spots. Maybe Dad had mentioned 'the blond poison' again! The contents of our packages got chopped up into smaller and smaller pieces. It is ridiculous to suspect that something was hidden in apples and lemons. Why chop them up in several pieces? I think it was just the fun of hurting us. Some of those young folks in G-3 were unable to control their emotions. I heard them say in front of some guards, "In the Nazi concentration camps prisoners had to be lured into gas chambers under false pretenses. If you had some here, we would go into them voluntarily. Be so humane and shoot us instead of treating us like trash with your unbearable harassments." To my surprise, those youngsters were not punished for their outbursts.

In November of 1952, great joy was bestowed on Inge and me. Among us was a music pedagogue, Ilse Rose, affectionately called "Röslein." She was a tiny lady with the sweetest personality. We all loved her! She approached Officer Reitz with the question of whether he would be kind enough to give his permission to form a chorus. He did. It was announced, and there was no lack of interested women. Otherwise, it was strictly forbidden to sing in Hoheneck. Don't ask me why—I don't know. Röslein had an incredible memory. She remembered not only great varieties of chorus music; but also the different voice parts. Her high soprano voice was as dear as a drop of fresh water. And there were many other remarkable, wonderful voices among us, some of them so low that they could easily sing tenor or bass, like Sonja von Rhaden with her full, rich, and warm, deep voice. Even the guards were impressed—we could see it in their faces. Most of them had never heard any high-quality chorus before, and that's what Röslein achieved. As small as she was, the second she raised her arms to conduct, one could have heard a pin drop, our attention was so focused. We also were very grateful to Officer Reitz.

Once in a great while, we were allowed to attend a denominational church service in Hoheneck's church. This must have been required in some old prison regulation because communists never go to any church. Our church in Hoheneck was big and beautiful. The largest oil painting behind the altar showed Jesus preaching with St. Peter and a large group of prisoners around him, some of them handcuffed. A Protestant pastor came for our very first church service. He had been told that most of us carried a twenty-five-year sentence because we were the worst criminals. Two of us had the chance to talk to him privately for a moment. They had informed him that most of us were there for a political or no reason at all. This white-haired pastor stood silently at the altar, while the organ was playing and just looked at us. What he saw were not the faces of criminals.

He saw faithful faces of educated ladies, some of them with white hair. "Dear Sisters," he began, and that did it. That was too much for us. Tears poured out of nearly every eye. He continued, "I find it hard to speak to you. I have never preached to so many faithful "ladies" in my church." He searched for words, but most of us did not hear much of what he said because we were crying so hard. The choir sang. Finally, it was time for the last prayer. The Catholics among us knelt, and everyone followed their example. All of us were so profoundly, deeply touched. The guards looked at us in great amazement. Most of them, I'll bet, never did go to church, being loyal Communists. The pastor, himself, also knelt, but his face was turned to us, not to the altar. Those of us who sat in the first few rows saw him crying. He never returned to Hoheneck. Another pastor, later, asked to see one of us. She was the mother of two sons who were in Bautzen prison as political inmates. He delivered greetings from the sons. One of the sons was Walter Kempowski, a famous author in later years.

We always so very much enjoyed whatever jumped over the big wall and came to us from the outside, like the pastors. The people of Stollberg knew from discharged criminals, who had finished their relatively short sentences, that the great majority of us were there for political reasons. For Christmas and New Year's, a large brass band from Stollberg delighted us every year with a long-lasting brass concert. They stood outside of our big wall, but in a private garden. Therefore, the police were unable to chase them away. Can you imagine how much we delighted in these concerts? They revealed so much of the compassion for us that was offered completely voluntarily by the Stollbergers.

Both our chorus rehearsals and our performances of actual concerts in our church were a great delight and pleasure for us. We practiced with great passion and enthusiasm, hoping to lift our comrades out of their daily, dull-gray life for an hour or two on the wings of music, into another sphere. I often remembered words of my beloved grandmother: "It is incomparably more enriching and fulfilling to give away love and joy than to receive them." True words, indeed. Not everyone can feel this, but I am grateful that I can. Otherwise, so much genuine beauty and true depth of life would be missing.

After a small Advent concert, we began practicing for a larger Christmas Concert. Several choir members remembered Christmas songs, and Röslein composed the other voice parts for those. It turned out magnificently; indeed, even the guards clapped along with the never-ending applause. We had to repeat this concert three times for those who did not, or could not, sign up for the first and second ones, and many who wanted to hear it again. It was very heartwarming and rewarding for us singers. This was the best Christmas I experienced in Hoheneck.

We also had a Christmas church service, and they showed us a film. Those activities helped us not to get lost too much in memories about Christmases at home. Another joy for us was that we were allowed to see photos of our families if they had sent any, not knowing that the administration would not give them to us, contrary to Sachsenhausen. Now they handed them to us to look at, like a big special Christmas present, for two days only. But like the remarkable, outstanding former German Chancellor Bismarck once said, "A companion of a buttered sandwich is often a cane." Too much brotherly love for bad convicts: that should be avoided. It should be distributed by milligrams. Therefore, the examination of our Christmas packages, in front of our eyes, was stricter than ever before. The latest rules were: no chocolate, no nuts, no figs. The ridiculous explanation was that something forbidden could be hidden in a nutshell or a fig. None of us had any doubt who enjoyed all the chocolate, nuts and figs. Nothing was returned to the families, who had not been informed about these brand new rules on time. If there is no plaintiff, no judge is needed. Our families found out about this in our January letter, provided it was not cut or blackened out. Any complaint would have ended up in some trash basket, anyway. But to be fair, 1953 was no doubt the easiest year in Hoheneck. We could kick the boots and foot rags to hell and wear socks and leather shoes; Inge her brown ones and I, my green ones. From April on, we were allowed to write and to receive twenty lines instead of fifteen.

We were permitted to practice and perform concerts and small plays, written by the talented ones among us. This was the time when we received gymnastic instructions and played volleyball. Thanks to

Commandante Officer Reitz, we could, for the first time, get books out of Hoheneck's library. And Inge and I were now given another job.

In late fall of 1952, they had enough nails, so we became knitting needle producers for knitting machines, which was much easier work. The long needles had to be perfectly straight. We achieved that on anvils, with small hammers.

We were (I have no idea why) the favorite workgroup of Officer Hammer, who was otherwise hated by everyone else. Maybe, we found out; he liked our very nice group leader, Betty Auerwald. He never mistreated anyone of our team, allowing us to write a special extra letter home, not just for the most productive ones but for all of us.

After the collapse of communism, former Hoheneck inmates used to have reunions for two or three days, once a year. Living in Pennsylvania and teaching German full time, I could never attend. At these occasions, the Stollberg brass band or its successors always played in the Hoheneck Church and at a stone memorial marker outside of the wall. This band also played there for many years, until the last political inmates were gone. Engraved on the memorial marker are all the names of our comrades who did not survive Hoheneck's abuse, including Gerda Schumacher and Gerdi Schulze, my dear and admired bunk neighbor in Sachsenhausen. Gerdi died in February of 1955, three months before Inge was amnestied.

The Hoheneck guards were looking for some volunteers to paint walls. They selected all politicals with a twenty-five-year sentence. At that time, we saw nothing suspicious in that. Much later, we found out why. For better and more food, Gerdi volunteered. None of us knew that the police considered us to be good enough guinea pigs to find out whether or not some old wall paint was poisonous. It was! No guard stayed in those rooms where the painters painted. All the painters eventually died of the same lung disease. Gerdi's parents, just like Gerda Schumacher's parents, as well as the parents of Heinz Blumenstein, Hans Bartel, Nethe and others, received the same wrong information about their children's cremation, and that no urns were available. The truth was that outside of the prison walls of Hoheneck, Bautzen, Sachsenhausen, and other Soviet prisons and camps, sixty-five thousand skulls and skeletons were dug up after 1989.

Needing something that they could lovingly and physically care for, my parents decided on honeybees and chickens. Dad built a chicken house with a large, open run area in our big back yard so that Mom could get a proud rooster. I have a picture of him—and several chickens. Dad went to the library and learned everything about beekeeping and how to build good bee houses, which eventually occupied another part of our back yard. Each swarm of his bees had individual, movable beehives. He could take them at night, when all the bees were inside, and drive them out of town, where certain flowers were growing. When he opened the little gates in the early morning, those incredibly hardworking insects collected this particular nectar, which gave the honey different tastes. At that time, I don't think that the German people outside were hungry anymore. Germany never had slums, but even eight years after the war ended, certain things were still difficult to find in East Germany. Mom's eggs and Dad's honey came in handy for bartering.

In September of 1953, we received another short but tremendously appreciated gift from Officer Reitz. We all were given two weeks of total freedom within the big outer wall during daylight hours. All dayrooms, cell doors, and building doors remained unlocked. We could not believe that, at first. If not working, we were able to enjoy fresh air anytime. We could visit friends from other buildings. This was, I suppose, much too generous and lion-hearted for mostly political prisoners, i.e. anti-communists. East Berlin Soviet headquarters were informed and stopped it immediately. This was a short but most lovely interlude, anyway. We correctly guessed that so much generosity would not last long, so we thoroughly enjoyed it as much as possible. It was in October of 1953 when our lovely interlude ended, and overnight, the tables were turned one hundred eighty degrees. Officer Reitz was replaced. Stalin died in 1953, and the free world hoped for changes, but it hoped in vain.

West Germany's industrial and economic situation had been blossoming enormously with generous help from the USA, France, and England; so much so that President Konrad Adenauer offered rubles to the Soviet Union to buy the political prisoners' freedom. The Soviets gladly took all the money, but who did they send home? Mostly criminals who had attacked a Soviet or had stolen some Soviet property or goods. However, a few politicals were lucky enough to be chosen. In November 1953, German newspapers published all that in letters, including names. Hoheneck got a newspaper once in a while for us to read. Usually we did not bother because it only consisted of anti-West, Communist propaganda. But one day, this paper hit us like a bomb. German men, who had been chief offenders like spies, returned home from Siberia. Their wives, sisters, etc. were involved in these cases and sentenced. They were among us in Hoheneck, but there was no discharge of "twenty-fivers." These women wrote application after application to talk to the new chief for weeks. Not a single answer from him. Those women whose husbands were home, now, exploded, understandably. In Siberia, the well-known counting-off Soviet system was practiced one, two, three, four, five, you go home, which is no system, no logic at all. Later, Inge and I experienced precisely the same thing: same arrest day, same age, same accusation, same twenty-five-year sentence, but Inge was amnestied six months before I was. No one was happier about that than I because shortly before, Inge had to face the terrible loss of her father.

The abuse by the guards increased from week to week. More and more often, we lived through searches of cells, dayrooms, and naked bodies. No one could have been more furious than all of us. When our families learned about the homecoming of prisoners with twenty-five years from Siberia, they were full of hope that we would follow. They bombarded the Soviet and East German authorities with endless demands. Everything landed in wastepaper baskets. What else? No answers!

The Soviets always instructed their obedient, cowering East German puppets about what to do and what not to do, and permitted them no decision-making powers. And the Soviets never listened to any suggestions. Our families didn't know that.

Hoheneck resembled a highly explosive, ticking bomb. We all sympathized with these women whose husbands were home and pictured ourselves in their places. Then Inge and I were personally affected. Klaus

Niepmann, our classmate and the chief leader of the Frankfurt/Oder spy groups, returned home from Siberia. Finally, the bomb exploded. Not actively at all, but, as the opposite, passively. No one ever knew where the first spark had been lit, or who first had the idea.

But this first spark had enormous consequences. In just a few hours, everyone knew about it, and everyone participated. The cell house had the knocking system from wall to wall and by heating pipes from the cellar to the attic. The communication from and to the dayrooms was done by sign language, which several of us knew. This was no problem. The dayrooms and-and upper cells had no shutters, just iron bars. The last attempt was made to speak to the chief. No answer! Then the hunger strike.

Even the sick and pregnant wanted to participate. Inmate nurses were able to prevent that because it would have meant death for several tuberculosis patients. On the morning of October 18, 1953, we got up at the usual time, around 6:00 A.M. We made our beds extra carefully but did not speak if a guard was near. We only whispered to each other, which created a very unusual silence. The guards sensed that something was brewing, but when they asked what was wrong, the answer was "Nothing" along with a shrug of shoulders. To make sure, there was a guard in the washroom on this day, but here also: silence. We sat down at our seat at the tables: silence. We accepted the coffee but did not pick up our breakfast of bread, margarine, jam, and sugar. The answer to the question "Why?" was I am not hungry today. When the same thing happened at lunch, the guards filled the bowls with soup themselves, and we were ordered to pick them up. Now the full bowls were sitting in front us, but no one touched her spoon. Still: silence. They were very upset, disturbed, and uneasy, but helpless. They had never experienced such an unbelievable amount of unity, solidarity, and conformance. We tried, but unsuccessfully, to persuade the older women to eat; none did. The police fetched a superior guard who commanded us to eat—no change. All this was a total, complete surprise for them. Not a single informer among us had mentioned a word to them. From now on, each guard was wearing a rubber truncheon on her belt.

It did not matter that all of a sudden, they offered us much better food, freshly cooked food with some meat. We one thousand two hundred politicals plus the prisoners who had been sentenced by German courts and had political sentences continued to refuse food. We were pleasantly surprised by the informers. Were they afraid of being beaten to a pulp during the night? But I think anyone would have been honestly ashamed to touch food. All former quarrels had vanished; foes became comrades, standing side by side firmly. The police read in an old instruction book. If a prisoner does not eat, he/she must lie down. Being in the dayroom at that time, Inge and I were taken to our attic. No one would have refused to work, not to give them any reason to accuse us of work-refusal, but their solution was the better one; we could rest. We rejoiced about the great financial loss for Hoheneck, i.e., the government's loss from the quite profitable sewing department.

All this had to be reported to headquarters, and the reaction followed on the spot! The old prison rules were outdated; the opposite was supposed to be done now. The new doctrine: Punish them hard! They took us back to our G-l dayroom, and hell began. There were frequent *Razzias* (body searches in cells, and dayrooms). If someone received a package, the contents were chopped into the smallest pieces and mixed them, making much of it inedible. We had to stand in the inner courtyard, three or four feet apart for an endlessly long time. One older woman collapsed. No one cared until finally, some of us were ordered to carry her to her cell. When she fell, a guard said, "It's all your own fault."

Another group of officers came and commanded us to eat. No change. After dark, I heard voices from the cell house over the courtyard. "Are you accepting any food?" The answer: "Not a crumb." But there was no provocation of any one of us, no violation of any rule. We had to line up for a roll call countless times a day, just for the harassment. They changed many of us from cell to dayroom and vice versa, hoping to break up cliques. Many of us had to go to hearings where they had endless questions to answer. The administration was most eager to find the instigators. They did not. After this extra food had been sitting on our table in front of us for a long time, we had to return it and dump it in a large container—for the pigs.

On the third day, they told us, "Whoever does not eat does not need to drink," and these subhuman creatures shut off all water. In the cell house, they had to accept coffee (only). But for the dayrooms came a little angel, fluttering down to us in the form of a male guard who worked with a few criminal convicts outside of the big wall. He was some heating specialist. He must have considered this no-water treatment as subhuman. He came with his female prisoner assistant into the attics to check something in the heating system. But he turned away from the heating and chatted for quite a while with us. During this time, his assistant showed some of us how to get some water out of the heating system.

After they had gone, we drew some water, let it cool, and drank it. No one got sick from it. Besides the help to relieve our thirst, we rejoiced in knowing that there were, indeed, compassionate people among the guards, like our blond angel had been. Still today, it seems like a miracle to me how one thousand three hundred women in different buildings were able to achieve such enormous solidarity for three days. The women who were fetched to hearings told them that the goal of the strike was not 'freedom' for us, but to speak to a Soviet officer about those now-free members of anti-Soviet organizations. He came, and one of us who spoke Russian was allowed to speak with him. His answer was, 'He'll look into that.' He probably never did, but we all ate on day four. Our basic goal had been achieved. East German authorities had zero influence on any amnesty. These were solely Soviet prerogatives from Moscow. A woman was amnestied who the Hoheneck police considered an obstinate, unworthy fascist. She was in *Karzer* for back-talking a guard. Moscow ignored the German objection, and she went home. On the other hand, the Germans suggested an informer (loyal communist) for amnesty, but Moscow ignored them.

The most enriching praise-worthy outcome of the strike (and not just during our hunger strike but in general) was that wonderful sense of belonging together, that loyalty among us, the loyalty and cooperation to that common cause, and the trustworthy, true and honest comradeship when it counted. Fights among us vanished for the good of a common cause. I remember all those many hours when we sat together, embroidering doilies, crocheting, knitting, singing, telling of our former free life or listening to those of us who had had eventful, interesting lives, like Sister Margarete. We comforted each other or gave each other hope. Those great hours are dearer in my memory than the endless harassments.

After we ate again, and most of us went to work, the entire affair was passé for us, but not for the police. They continued hearings, and they had to report to East Berlin Headquarters that they had punished the culprits. Inge and I had always followed our rule to disappear in a crowd, never to speak up. Not all of us were wise enough to do this. Those were fished out now and sent to the Brandenburg Prison. Among them was our innocent Röslein, a first-class, outstanding leader, but only in music. She could not kill a mosquito! Never again was there any music in Hoheneck.

Shortly after our strike, one of our loved-by-all ladies, Hilde Nehring, went home. She had finished her seven-year political sentence by a German court. She had also memorized the addresses of our families, and now the world got to know what Hoheneck was. All visits were watched by guards who were never the friendliest ones but to the contrary. Our families had no idea how these bitches behaved in our daily life, Hilde enlightened them at home.

Twenty months had passed since the last visit of our family members. Finally, the Soviets "graciously" dropped the visitation prohibition for us twenty-five-year spies, the scum of all prisoners. In November of 1953, we unexpectedly received an application for a visit, still only one family member. We were just as delighted as our parents. Our fathers intended to come, but my letters had revealed my great worry about my mother, who had suffered dangerous heart problems. My deep concerns had kept me awake at night. The thought of never again seeing one of my parents was simply unbearable. It was Inge who had to suffer through this unimaginable pain, two years later.

To show me that Mom had recovered well from her illness, our parents changed the plans: our mothers came. This event started a chain of visits to which a new link was added every three months. It was good that no one knew about the eight more links to be added for me.

December of 1953 was so warm that roses were said to be blooming outside. If we were lucky to get a friendly guard for our *Rundgang,* we did not wear a jacket. We rolled up our shirt sleeves and did not wear any socks. A warm Christmas seemed to be heading in our direction. But one never knows what St. Peter has in mind. On December 23, the temperatures dropped a lot. Next day, the German Christmas Day, the ground was covered with the first snow. We were delighted. But we did not like the Christmas tree which suddenly stood in the center of the courtyard. We saw it as a mockery of our present condition, and the cell house did not see the electric lights being turned on in the evening, anyway. Maybe it was not mockery, but some very rare humane intention. None of us wanted to see this reminder of former at-home Christmases. This Hoheneck was no longer Sachsenhausen!

After the first snow, Father Winter did not withdraw from his territory anymore. Beginning in January of 1954, some guards dropped remarks now and then, about major amnesties. Nothing happened for a while, but then the first prisoners were allowed to go home. All had lower sentences until Waltraud Schmidt was called. She was from Frankfurt/Oder and had been sentenced to twenty-five years in our Potsdam trial. Werner Niepmann, also sentenced to twenty-five years, the brother of Klaus and founder of the Frankfurt group, came home from Siberia. Dieter Linke, (another twenty-five year political who was Inge's former boyfriend (and later husband) was amnestied, to Inge's great delight. But bureaucracy usually proceeds at the speed of a sloth. Soon the amnesties stopped, started again in 1955, then stopped again for several months.

Inge and I were very happy indeed for each woman who had the great pleasure of going home. We were not envious, just disappointed that our names still were not called. But like making nail heads, many blows are necessary to produce the best steel! Destiny is not the most significant and character-forming force for me. More important is whether or not one has the strength, willpower, and determination to create inner fate, i.e., growth, by using outer, worldly happenings.

If I try to find a meaning for all that happens to me, nothing tragic overwhelms me. I believe that there is a reason for all that happens to us, but a human being is much too insignificant to recognize it.

When both of our fathers came to visit us in Hoheneck on February 10, 1954, Inge and I were unemployed for a little while. The straightening of knitting needles turned out to be not profitable enough. They needed help in the kitchen, and we volunteered. For some unknown reason, they never forced us yet, to do any work. In the kitchen, we peeled potatoes and cleaned vegetable, which were something nice on which to chew. Besides that, once in a while, some criminals who worked in the main kitchen brought us little pieces of meat or something good to eat. After this rather short interlude, we worked on bales of different fabrics, searching for any irregularities which we repaired, when possible, or marked their presence with chalk. We learned the art of invisible darning. This turned out to be useful in later life, to be practiced on my husband's, my friends and my clothes, as well.

Our work crew, inspecting bales of fabric, was no longer needed; or else the administration had figured out that sewing was a more profitable business for Hoheneck's coffers. Amnesties had stopped for quite a long time, and in July of 1954, came the end of "volunteering for work." All of us had to work. Inge and I became sewers. Half of the second floor of the north wing was remodeled from dayroom four into a sewing factory with hundreds of electric sewing machines. The pants, blouses, aprons, etc. produced there went to government-owned stores, which usually had been tricked out of private hands like my Dad's was later. As sewers, we were harassed and aggressively pushed to produce more and more and more to meet or exceed the high given norm; it was true exploitation for no pay.

Those among us who knew sewing construction began teaching others, but there was not much to teach, because all of us worked in an assembly line. If my task was shoulder seams, that was it: fifty, one hundred, five hundred shoulder seams. The more skillful ladies of us may have had to put pockets into pants or fit collars or sleeves into blouses. Everyone worked under constant pressure because we depended on the work before us, like a never-ending chain. Everyone had a high quota. Those who underachieved their quota were changed to a different machine with a simpler task. But those who managed to exceed their quota received little extra rewards. These overachievers were allowed to buy cigarettes, candy, cookies, etc. in our little prison shop. Whoever managed to exceed the quota excessively got an extra letter home. After time passed by, the Soviets ordered the East Germans to pay us something for any productive work which they sold. We received a few pennies for a day's work. The machine noise never stopped in twenty-four hours. Not only did the guards harass us, but fellow prisoners also did as well because they desperately wanted to get some award. I was never good enough for an award during my eighteen months as a sewer, eventually trying all three of the shifts. But instead, I had a different goal. I figured out how I could use this work as a real learning experience. That was relatively easy; other women had the same idea. The guards had no objection and did not care at all if we exchanged machines and tasks. One of them once asked me why I did that. I told her, "I think I can achieve a higher quota on this different task." I learned how to sew complete blouses, trousers, aprons, jackets, etc. Many decades later, after my husband had passed away, I entertained myself at home, after my teaching responsibilities were completed, by sewing my summer clothes and doing minor jobs and alterations for friends.

One day, a most tragic accident happened. One of us dropped the bobbin of thread that belonged in her machine. Edeltraut Eckert, our mechanic (prisoner) came to help and to retrieve the bobbin that had fallen into the machine. She did not stop the electric current on the machine, which was a requirement. She saw the bobbin and thought she could get it. But a moving leather band caught some of her hair and in a second, scalped half of her head. The scalp was packed in disinfected ice, and Edeltraut was rushed to the Stollberg Hospital. In a day or two, she was transported to a larger hospital in the big city of Leipzig. All attempts to transplant the scalp failed. She died, all alone, of tetanus. We all mourned for her. She was a kind and loved comrade, whose beautiful poems many of us had memorized. Edeltraut died on the same day we had to part with our beloved linden tree in the courtyard. It was stolen from us!

When both of our fathers came to visit us in Hoheneck, on May 17. 1954, none of any of us had any idea that this was the very last time, for both of them, to drive up the steep hill to our fortress, for two very tragic reasons. Ten weeks later, in July, my Dad himself ended up behind bars, because the Communist East German government was anxious to get ownership of his booming business and his real estate. Besides, Dad would never, ever (which was what they asked of him) be an informer. For a long time, he had been a thorn in the Communists' eyes. He did not belong to the Communist Party. He wrote innumerable pleas for clemency for me to Berlin and Moscow (an aunt of mine spoke Russian)

But most important of all, he was still a very successful independent businessman and real estate owner. He refused their repeated attempts to degrade him to 'director' of his firm without any ownership. Communism in East Germany did not go as far as in the Soviet Union, where they dictatorially disowned all independent businessmen. The East Germans used different methods to achieve their goal. They used informers, but who knew who they were? Two of those had no problem having Dad arrested and sentenced and disowned. One of them—informer number one—told Dad that a customer of Dad's was on a list to be arrested for connection with a politician in West Berlin. Dad never missed a chance to help somebody. He promptly went to his customer, who was informer number two, and warned him. This evil bastard took Dad's identification (by law, nobody was allowed in public without that) and handed it to the STASI (East German Secret Police). Early the next morning, the STASI arrested Dad and turned our home upside down without finding anything incriminating. Dad had even warned informer number one not to spread forbidden news. But, of course, he did not report him to the STASI, and that was the reason for sentencing him to two years in prison. It revealed Dad's anticommunist attitude, they said. As mentioned before, the true reason was the expropriation of his business and real estate. In his sentence, he was also labeled "dishonored person" which meant, after his imprisonment, he was not permitted to do any other work but street cleaning for the following five years. But what worried Dad most of all was my mother. Badly crippled with arthritis, always weak, now she was alone. It is a true miracle to me how she possibly managed to handle everything on her own.

Mom sent me my monthly package filled with the best, first-class food. She sent the same to Dad. She took care of her chickens and Dad's bees. She lived off the rental income of her own apartment house where she lived. Family and friends contributed generously to the packages, even my former Latin teacher.

Dr. Hutloff and his wife sent cervelat sausages. The chocolates of my Godfather, Mom's brother, were never missing; neither was the hard salami from a close friend of our family, Uncle Oskar. Even neighbors dropped off something for the packages. Superintendent Wachholz collected 500 marks for her in his church and often visited her, offering his help. But with her crippled hands, it was she who had to weigh each item for the packages, wrap them, pack them, add the weight of the packing material, and carry them by streetcar to the post office.

I did not have any idea about all this. Mom did not mention one word in her letters, and she found clever, believable words in her letters and during her visits in Hoheneck, explaining the reason for this, that she was all alone. Dad could not write anything in her letters to me. She wanted to spare me from the truth as long as possible and invented stories that Dad was traveling, visiting relatives, etc. After some time without a single word written by Dad, I became suspicious. Mom went to the parents of the three Schulze sisters, whose oldest, Ingeborg, was the most mature of us. It was she who had jumped out of the second-floor window in Potsdam. Mom wanted her to break the bad news to me orally, as gently as possible. Ingeborg did. Of course, I was upset and despaired that I was doomed not to be able to help Mom in any way. I did not want any more packages, but Mom did not listen to me. Dad always had robust health; he was never sick. Therefore, I was glad that his sentence was only two years. He surely could survive that, if Mom could. A superhuman will power, determination, and faith enabled her to do so.

Dad's arrest was not the last blow for us; a much more tragic one followed. In November of 1954, Inge was unexpectedly taken to the front office. There, some guard told her in the most unsympathetic manner possible, "Your father died and has been buried. Now, return where you belong, Number 2222." Inge turned to stone, did not cry, but could not quite comprehend what she had just been told.

She came back to dayroom G-3, where we lived at that time, went to her bed, buried her head and sobbed uncontrollably. I cried myself, seeing her unbearable grief. The only thing I thought might be a tiny bit helpful was to keep everybody away from her bed. She never had an enemy. She was loved by all, and many wanted to express their condolences. Some even brought small gifts for her. He had died of kidney disease, Inge learned from her mother's next letter. After her amnesty, six months later, she also found out that her Dad, on his deathbed, had begged again and again to see Inge for the last time, to see her, without even speaking to her. What do you expect of a Communist bureaucracy with a total lack of compassion and sympathy? When our Moms came visiting us in March 1955, they told us in more detail about Dad's arrest and Mr. Pietsch's death. I was glad that both mothers traveled together. It was a pity that none knew, not even the police that Inge would be a free woman in merely two months.

April and May brought a few more amnesties. On May 5, 1955, it was Inge's turn. I had prayed for that so hard because after her Dad's recent death I did not want to see her left behind after any amnesty for me. We had just returned to our G-3 after a night shift. Inge had pulled her blanket over her face and was deep asleep. I woke her up and told her, "Get up, you go home. We have to wrap your belongings into the blanket."

She opened her eyes and responded, "How about you?"

"I shall join you soon," I said but did not believe it, because of the Soviet system one, two, three, four, five . . . you go, as mentioned before. I was correct. Almost eight months passed, and they were not the easiest months in Hoheneck. I saw her walk to the shower house, where they shed all of their prison clothing. In another room, they received private clothing, and I saw her one more time when she was walking with a few other women towards the big gate that led to freedom. She turned around, looked up at our G-3, and we waved to each other for the last time. I was alone and felt as if I had lost a limb of my body.

At that time, each amnestied woman had a choice as to whether she wished to be discharged to East Germany or West Germany. Many families had left East Germany because at that time the wall had not been built, (not until 1961). Inge and her mother had decided that Inge should immediately go to West Berlin and her mother and sister would follow. Her mother knew that Inge would have excellent prospects and assistance in West Germany, but she would always remain an outcast in the east. How true. I found out.

I pictured Inge to be a happy, free woman, enjoying life, maybe dating, enjoying social life again, without serious worries. But this was far from the truth. She found it depressingly difficult to face a world so drastically different from eight years ago in Frankfurt/Oder. It was very hard for her to adjust to all those demands of freedom. *Not* only that all people dressed so very differently (the fashion had changed), but suddenly there was decision-making required. This was non-existent for so many years, we just obeyed. Financially she had no problems. The West Berlin government gave her a generous amount of money on which to live. They classified her as a political "victim of terror," and this passport opened many doors for her, later also for me. It was too dangerous for her to ride a train from West Berlin to West Germany. The train could have an engine problem at any time; then East German police would enter the train and pull out anyone whom they considered suspicious. Inge would have been among those because she had violated East German law simply by leaving East Germany, her original home.

West Berlin took no chances; they flew her to West Germany. She had expressed the wish to take the *Abitur,* the final high school exam, which in Germany is equivalent to the American College Entrance Exam. Inge could not possibly take this very difficult exam, which we had started but never finished in 1947 due to arrest. This was eight years ago. Inge was not the only one in this mishap situation. Therefore, the West German government had made arrangements for those Soviet victims. A Lutheran Church provided comfortable free housing and food in the city of Wuppertal, and a Senior High School offered free classes and review workshops. All teachers volunteered without pay. After six months and intensive private lessons by the faculty, the students were ready to take the Abitur Exam. Inge passed the exam and matriculated at the University of Cologne, where Dieter Linke also was studying. Finally, they got married and had a happy family: two children and grandchildren. Inge is still alive, living with her daughter's family.

About one month after Inge relished her first breath of freedom, a day came that surprised me, too, with great happiness. Besides the first letter from my parents, the first package with almost forgotten delicacies, the first visit of my parents, a most significant event delighted me. A guard took me to our church which also served as an assembly room. The small group of us was informed that the government—in reality the Soviets, most graciously had reduced our twenty-five sentences. Mine was no longer twenty-five but nine years. The paperwork seemed to be binding and honest, and we had to sign for having received the new sentence. But I still had a problem believing in the overwhelming new situation. I returned to my day room G-3 and doubted about the reductions, but others convinced me that this could not possibly be a malicious game of the East Germans. But still, I found it difficult to grasp the fact that I should indeed go home to Mom in about fifteen months. Fifteen months are a trifle compared to the almost eight years that I had survived in cruel incarceration, especially in Hoheneck. I counted the remaining days again: sixty-four more weeks, four hundred forty-eight more days, and the next day it would be four hundred forty-seven. And how fast one day went by, working on a sewing machine, especially at night shifts, 10:0 P.M. to 6:00 A.M. There would be twenty-one-night shifts for me. I wanted to find a piece of paper and draw a calendar with four hundred forty-eight days so that I could cross off one each day. But, I decided that this was not necessary at all, because the decreasing number of days was so indistinguishably, non-erasably, constantly in my mind. During my night shifts, around 12:00 A.M., I could hardly wait for the clock hand to pass the twelfth hour.

I would not go home in 1972, maybe after my parents' death, but in fifteen months. I was no longer interested in any amnesties. I did not begrudge those lucky ones who would go home tomorrow or next week. I could not have cared less that I had to move back into the cell house because of more expansion of the profitable tailoring factory. When all September packages from home were canceled, I thought good, so Mom has one burden less on her shoulders. She continued to send packages to Dad. From now on, I viewed all my life like sitting in a theater, watching some play. Each one of my days resembled a scene in the play, and after the last scene, in October of 1956, I would go home from that theater, and see and hug my parents.

Mom's visits had lost most of the sorrowful feelings about being alone. We made plans about what we would do after my homecoming. Dad would be home then, also. We carefully speculated what he might want to do, but we had to circumvent this point in front of the guard. The goodbyes at the end of Mom's visits lost their stinging pain.

Christmas of 1955 was the most horrible one in all of my life, except 1947 in Potsdam. I was glad that Inge did not have to live through it. The Hoheneck guards did everything imaginable to mistreat us and to make our lives as miserable as they could. Maybe they were furious that so many politicals had been amnestied by Moscow, and they could do absolutely nothing to prevent that. To them, we were more despicable than the worst criminals, even murderers. They had been brainwashed well! Their ghastly treatments were saturated with the vilest hatred. The cell in which they had put me had two single beds and was intended for two inmates. They stuffed seven of us into it. When we seven returned from our sewing shift, both beds had been removed. Without any straw sacks on the first night we were lying on the concrete floor lined up like sardines. I considered myself lucky not to lie next to "Mr. Potty." When they removed the beds, they carried out a thorough *Razzia* for forbidden items. They found my two-inch pencil, but they had found so many items in our and other cells that they told us that punishment for all of those would take place after Christmas. It never did because too many items had been found. Another devious mistreatment without any reason at all: they collected all bedsheets. We had to lie on the dirty straw sacks over Christmas. The minutes of *Rundgang* we so irritating because of the guards' constant screaming, that we gladly returned to our cells. But we were forced to send a gift package to our families with candy, perfume, or bathroom items, etc. purchased in the little shop, to show the world outside how thoughtful and generous Hoheneck was. We viewed this as nothing but mockery. I wonder what our families were thinking at that time after Hilde Nehring had informed them about the true conditions and treatments after Officer Reitz.

Mom had sent me another one of those pretty face cloths in my Christmas package. For some unknown reason, the time before Christmas was always a time for the most frequent, unexpected body, cell, and day-room searches. I detected a piece of some paneling starting to bend away from the wall in the sewing room. In an unwatched moment (the guards were usually sitting in the comfortable, warm guards' room), I pulled that piece of paneling a bit further, stuffed my face cloth behind it, and hammered the paneling tight to the wall with my fists. I intended to retrieve it after Christmas, but I had no chance because I was amnestied on December 28, 1955. I wonder if the face cloth is still behind the paneling?

I did everything that they asked with a smile, knowing that this was my very last Hoheneck Christmas. I just registered the subhuman behavior of those subhuman creatures in their blue uniforms. I expected only ten more months under their scourge. I had no idea that it was only for ten days.

German Christmas in 1955 was a Saturday, i.e., Monday was still a German Christmas holiday (December 26) and Tuesday (December 27) a full workday. My shift was 2:00 A.M. until 10:00 A.M., but at 10:00 A.M. I was not at my machine anymore.

After this most unpleasant Christmas, not one of us had much energy to achieve a lot. We received a few pennies per hour of work. They made so much money on our labor and yet treated us like dirt. On the other hand, I figured that time would go by faster if I concentrated on sewing the blouse into which I had to fit the sleeves. After about two hours of work, a leading guard came and called my name and told me to bring "all my belongings." That was my jacket. I buttoned it properly to avoid rebuke. My first thought was my little pencil which they had found in the *Razzia*. Christmas was over, and I guessed that they started to punish the "sinners." I also thought that taking my pencil was ironic and undeserved punishment because I just had used this pencil to make somebody very happy. Brigitte Grünke from Frankfurt/Oder, a pharmacist and very kind lady almost my age, had received the usual twenty-five-year sentence in Potsdam at our trial. Her sentence, like mine was reduced. She would go home two months after me. I was able to find a sturdy piece of paper. With my little pencil I drew a calendar on it that ended with Brigitte's homecoming day. Each little block sported the number of days of her remaining incarceration. She was delighted to cross off the blocks, day by day. The monumental task for me was how to get it to her. My guardian angels helped me. We had a Christmas church service in our beautiful church. Brigitte, being a pharmacist, worked in our prison infirmary. The nurses of the infirmary were in the church before us, but I was able to mingle with other inmates and made it to where the infirmary prisoners sat without any guard noticing my "violation."

Brigitte got my calendar. She did not have to cross out many days. She was amnestied from Moscow, shortly after me, and had decided to be discharged to West Berlin.

I do have guardian angels! A few months ago, I catapulted over the railing from upstairs in my house, when I had a terrible cold that left me half-blind from swollen and watering eyes. I landed on a couch next to the steps, bounced off the couch, and landed downstairs on the floor. Not even one bone was broken, not one muscle or tendon was pulled. My angels helped me with Brigitte and many times before when I had planned on making someone happy or aiding someone who needed help. If some insurmountable object blocked my way, and I had no idea how to remove that obstacle, someone always showed up for my rescue. In spite of all difficulties, I somehow succeeded.

Expecting to be marched into the *Karzer* for my pencil, I was pleasantly surprised that the guard took me to my cell. When I saw, now, that a few other prisoners were taken to their cells, I realized that I might have been amnestied. I was told to wrap all my belongings in my blanket (which was never done for *Karzer*). I had just barely enough time to embroider into a towel the name of Mrs. Hausler, who had lent me a sewing needle, a most precious, valuable possession. At work, nobody used a needle. We all did machine sewing only.

I stuck the needle next to her name and hoped that my cellmates returned it to Mrs. Hausler. My cellmates enjoyed all the food out of my packages and many plastic food containers. Their chances for any amnesty were small. They all had been sentenced recently by German courts, all of them for political reasons. However, the German courts did not give monster sentences of twenty-five years. When the guard fetched me, I saw ten or twelve other prisoners at the end of the hall with their blanket bundles. Only two of them, Katharina Patzold and Gerdi Koeck, had twenty-five-year Soviet sentences.

All of us were taken to the west wing. There was more paperwork and a few signatures, and then we were asked whether or not we intended to return to the same address where we had been arrested "in case we might" get amnestied. Several said that their family had moved to West Germany. Those were later discharged to West Berlin. I had no such choice. I wanted to return to Mom. We received straw sacks, but no sheet or pillow, and some food and spent the entire night waiting. Almost all of us stayed awake, full of anticipation. I did not. I could not have cared less whether I left there tomorrow or ten months later. I slept soundly on that dirty straw sack. I had miraculously survived six years in this side-chamber of hell. What did one or a few weeks more or less, matter?

The necessary discharge actions started the next day, December 28, 1955. This may have been the most important day of my life. We were taken to the wash house, took a shower, received superficial, perfunctory health exams, and then received the rest of our personal belongings, which had not been sent home years ago. I just got my dirty underwear from 1947 and surprise! Surprise! A telegram from Mom. It had arrived in Hoheneck four days ago but was not given to me. I still have it. It reads: "Congratulations on your homecoming." No family was informed about any amnesty of any family member returning home. (The Hoheneck administration did not know about who was going to be amnestied from Moscow several days in advance.) It was one of Mom's premonitions and presentiments that had told her in advance. They could not have asked Mom to send me clothes. This would have given away the top secret of my amnesty. I was given a plain brown dress, too large for me, with a button missing. It was badly wrinkled. I could not have cared less. I also received an ugly plain black, unlined summer topcoat in December! I had always been overlooked when they conducted hair-cutting procedures, just for fun and malice of the guards. One of us lost her beautiful, long blond braids, which she used to wear like a golden crown on top of her head.

My thin hair provoked no interest among the cutters at any time. Now a guard just stuffed it into the back of the topcoat and wound a dark blue scarf around my head. Of course, there was no mirror. Consequently, we had no idea how awful most of us looked. We had none or only a little bit of our upper wear left. We just giggled at each other's masquerade, after so many years of having seen almost nothing but dark gray and dark blue uniforms. They took us now to the east wing, the administration building, where we were finally informed about our amnesty, i.e. freedom. Nobody even had a small smile. We were scared. The very last thing that they handed to us was the official paper of our release, a small piece of paper the size of my hand if that big. It merely says that I was working for a certain sewing company, but nothing about amnesty.

I looked at it, and I wondered why nothing stirred inside of me. The others must have felt the same way. There was no joy in any of their faces. I could not comprehend, at all, my indifference toward this significant, small slip of paper which was the passport to my freedom. I may, perhaps, have just been afraid, afraid—this is unbelievable—to leave behind the safety, security, and relative lack of serious worries in Hoheneck. I had, a long time ago, managed to make the nasty behavior of the guards bounce off the invisible wall of granite that I had erected around myself. I was also afraid of all those innumerable challenges and demands of the free life out there. Dad was not home yet, Mom crippled with arthritis, always depending on help, and I, myself, without a job, without an *Abitur*, i.e., unable to apply at any university. There were so many insurmountable handicaps and worries awaiting me out there. I was hollow inside. I seemed to face an insurmountable precipice ahead of me. I let myself be carried by the current and shied away from thinking ahead.

Each of us received a small package of food and our train ticket. We had to use Hoheneck's prison bus with three guards to ride to the Stollberg train station. The police wanted to avoid the possibility of us walking into Stollberg and talking about the treatment in Hoheneck. A former school friend of Mom's, Mrs. Kaete Pemp, was married in Stollberg; our parents had always visited there. I knew the address and telephone number because I was supposed to go there, after a possible amnesty, and wait for Mom to come to pick me up and take me home.

I asked for that permission when they handed me my train tickets. Their response was obvious. I was not even permitted to call them.

The nearest larger train station near Stollberg was Chemnitz, about a half-hour away. Everyone else would travel from Chemnitz to Frankfurt/Oder the shortest distance of about two hours. But not I, oh no! This route leads to Frankfurt/Oder via Berlin. There would have been the possibility and temptation for me to leave my train in West Berlin. What a crime! This was called *Republikflucht* (escape from the Republic). It was punished by years of jail in East Germany. My prescribed long, long detour led me over Leipzig and Cottbus. In both cities, there was an endless waiting time for the connecting train, so that I arrived in Frankfurt/Oder after midnight.

We had received the "enormous" and most "gracious" sum of two dollars and fifty cents, which equaled at the time ten marks as travel cash. How generous! However, sixty or seventy years ago, you were able to buy more than today for that sum. They kept all of our earnings from our pay for sewing during December.

All of us bought something good to eat—hot dogs, cake, etc., at the railroad station. But I preferred to send two telegrams, instead, to Mom and Dad. There was even enough cash left to buy a new, long pencil and a tiny note pad to start my future diary. Of course, the tiny pencil stub, which had almost transported me into *Karzer,* reappeared in my mind.

By our appearance and the watching guards, the Stollbergers recognized where we came from. The guards were also watching that we all entered the train to Chemnitz. My feelings changed from minute to minute. I could not deny it, there was a certain, limited sentiment of security in the cell, and I did not seem to have quite enough courage, yet, to abandon it. But my feelings of cold feet, worries, and concerns were replaced by joy and delight that I was able to walk through the railroad station a free woman. Of course I was impatiently looking forward to holding Mom in my arms, which had never been permitted except for the very first visit. My comrades went to the stores inside the station, but we soon were huddled together again in a group of insecure, still rather timid women. The other people also knew that nearly all the women in Hoheneck were incarcerated for political reasons. They looked at us with great pity and compassion but kept their distance. Only one lady stepped up to me, asking if I knew her sister in prison, but I did not. This lady came to the station every time prisoners were amnestied, hoping to see her sister. The Stollbergers watched when a small bus with prisoners in civilian clothing left Hoheneck.

Finally, the time came to board the train to Chemnitz. Those of us who had chosen to go to West Berlin changed trains in Chemnitz and boarded the Berlin train. The rest of us changed to trains home or, like I, had endless waiting time for my train to Leipzig, followed by more long waiting time in Cottbus. Finally, long after midnight, I could achieve the last leg of the trip, my train to Frankfort/Oder. Katharina and Gerdi were still my travel companions, for a little while longer. Then I was alone, among very few other midnight travelers. I was no longer afraid. I realized, now fully, I was free like a bird in the air. My dad would have said, now, *"Frisch gewagt ist halb gewonnen"* ("A fresh, optimistic start, is half the winning").

In 1993, after the collapse of Stalin's brutal reign in the Soviet Union, everyone who had been sentenced by the S.M.T. (Soviet Military Tribunal) received a Russian document from Moscow. It stated that he/she was no longer listed in the Kremlin among the spies against the former Soviet Union. Does anyone ever believe Communists? There was no apology, not even some sort of sympathy was included for so many innocent people who had to suffer years of incarceration and mistreatment, or death.

Hoheneck Castle housed political prisoners at the outset of the Cold War.

Margarete Suttinger (née Müller) who
was the "nastiest" prison guard.

The chickens and beehives that occupied Helga's parents while she was in prison.

Inge had her parents send flowers for Helga's parents' 25th anniversary while Helga was in prison.

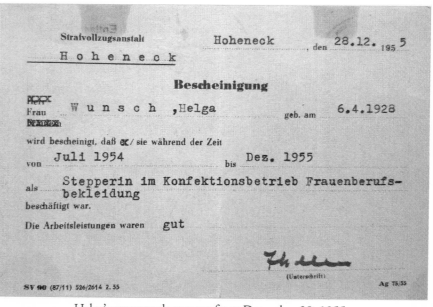

Strafvollzugsanstalt   Hoheneck   , den   28.12. 195 5

H o h e n e c k

Bescheinigung

Frau   W u n s c h , Helga   geb. am   6.4.1928

wird bescheinigt, daß er / sie während der Zeit

von   Juli 1954   bis   Dez. 1955

als   Stepperin im Konfektionsbetrieb Frauenberufs-
bekleidung
beschäftigt war.

Die Arbeitsleistungen waren   gut

(Unterschrift)

SV 90 (87/11) 526/2614 2.55   Ag 75/55

Helga's amnesty document from December 28, 1955.

Helga at 27 on December 28, 1955.

A reunion of inmates from Fanrkfurt-Oder circa 1990. Helga was unable to attend.

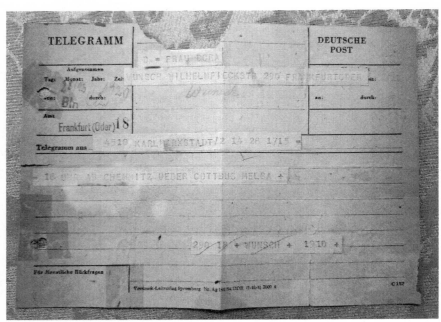

Telegram announcing Helga's return by train.

Inside Hoheneck, now a museum. If you touch the hands, they tell the incarceration story of this person.

EPILOGUE

AFTER HER amnesty, Helga returned to school to review for a final high school diploma. She was determined to get it since no higher education was possible without it. The East German government flatly refused, in 1956, to let her get any public school reviews, as she was regarded to have been a former "spy against Communism." She had to escape to West Germany where she received help and support. Six months later, she earned her high school diploma and matriculated to the Johann Wolfgang Goethe University in Frankfurt am Main where she received her German B. A. and M. A.

Later, a teaching position opened in Langen, near Frankfurt am Main, where here parents now lived.

A pen pal relationship with the American Karl Rist led to their marriage in 1961. Helga emigrated to Pennsylvania. Having been a passionate teacher, she taught German to senior high classes at Lower Dauphin High School in Hummelstown. After her salary reached a ceiling, she was handed a difficult schedule requiring her to teach six daily classes of German 1 in middle school. She resigned and transitioned to Wilson College where she taught German to college students. In 2004, she was promoted to Assistant Professor. Helga retired in 2006 following a disabling accident, ending 45 years of teaching.

For 12 more years, Helga actively volunteered for Hospice of Central Pennsylvania and the Harrisburg Symphony Orchestra. Helga continues to live in Camp Hill.

BIBLIOGRAPHY

Finn, Gerhard. *Die Frauen von Hoheneck*, Berlin, Germany, 25, 52, 73.
Müthel Eva. *Für dich blüht kein Baum*, Frankfurt, Germany.
Rist, Helga. Handwritten diaries.
Stern, Joachim. *Und der Westen schweigt*, Bonn, Germany.

INDEX

Made in the USA
Middletown, DE
11 April 2020